ICE DANCING

ICE DANCING

MONTY READHEAD

*Twice winner of the
Open Professional Ice Dancing
Championship of Great Britain.
Gold Dance, Gold Pair-Skating,
Inter-Gold Figure and Instructors Medals.
Chief Instructor at Nottingham Ice Stadium*

PELHAM BOOKS

First published in Great Britain by
PELHAM BOOKS LTD
26 Bloomsbury Street
*London, W.C.*1
1968

© 1968 *by Monty Readhead*

7207 0221 6

Set and printed in Great Britain by
Tonbridge Printers Ltd, Peach Hall Works, Tonbridge, Kent
in Baskerville eleven on fourteen point, and bound by
James Burn at Esher, Surrey

CONTENTS

ILLUSTRATIONS

DIAGRAMS

The author wishes to thank Messrs Thorburn &
Phillips, Nottingham, who took all the photographs reproduced in this book

Introduction

Since I wrote my first book there have been more Medal Tests introduced and a number of new dances; in fact there have been so many alterations and additions in recent years that this has caused considerable delay in producing this book. However, the Tests appear to be reasonably settled for the moment, hence I am venturing to bring you an up-to-date book of *Ice Dancing*.

As there are now two extra tests before reaching the Silver than there were at the time of my earlier book, I have decided to deal with Ice Dancing from the beginning up to, and including, the Silver Dance Test. This has enabled me to keep the book a manageable length. It is my hope to follow this book with one dealing with the Inter-Gold and Gold Dance Tests, and competitive skating.

In tackling the vast subject of Ice Dancing I feel it would be folly to approach it from any other angle than that of trying to discover the reason why so many people go on at exactly the same standard season after season, making it increasingly difficult for them to become really good dancers. *The longer you practice your faults – the longer it will take you to get out of them.* So repeatedly do they practice the same old faults acquired in the beginning of their dancing career, that my first task on undertaking to train a pupil to dance really well is to diagnose the root of his or her trouble.

It may surprise many people when I say that the fault can invariably be traced to their first day on ice. I will deal with this in Chapter One. So many skaters, by twisting the body into the most fantastic positions, manage to get themselves round a circle, forming a very poor interpretation of edges to centres, when they really cannot skate accurately forward and backward round the rink. The weight is never properly balanced on the skate and the performer consequently lurches on to the next edge instead of transferring the weight easily and striking off at precisely the same moment.

I therefore intend to work my way up from the beginning, giving a brief description of the best way to start skating and how to get the most out of a natural ability. First, in fact, to explain the *do's* and *don't's* up to the dancing stage, and then to try and help the more experienced dancer. I shall try to be explicit and drive even the smaller points home, rather than to go straight from A to B, leaving the reader to guess the rest – in other words, in the same way as I would instruct a pupil. Accuracy in all details will be the main essential.

I have drawn diagrams of all dances where I think it necessary, omitting those where the pattern is obvious and would be of little assistance to the dancer. Also, where necessary, I have drawn separate diagrams for the lady and the man. To save having too much writing on the diagrams I have not numbered the edges. The figures inside the diagram next to each edge represent the number of beats for that particular edge, the letters on the outside describing the edge; R.F.O. – Right Forward Outside. Likewise, in the Rocker Foxtrot, L.F.O.R.B.O. – Left Forward Outside Rocker Backward Outside.

The book is also illustrated by photographs, some showing the correct position and others the wrong position. In order to have these taken at precisely the right moment, most have been taken with little or no movement, hence the lack of action apparent in some. The reason for this is, for example, the lady's free leg on the fourth edge in the Foxtrot, if taken at the wrong angle, would not show the lady's free leg position to the best advantage in either the right or wrong position. Even at slow speeds the photographs have to be taken with split second timing. Where possible, however, full action has been shown.

The photographs are of myself and my wife with whom I won the National Skating Association of Great Britain *Open Professional Ice Dancing Championship*. I would like to place on record my sincere thanks to my wife for partnering me for the photographs and for her invaluable help throughout the writing of this book.

CHAPTER ONE

What to do and what not to do
Before Learning to Dance

On entering an ice rink the first thought of a beginner is to get a pair of skates and make his début on the ice. Many think it a waste of money to have a lesson until they are able to forward and backward skate. This is a pity as the over enthusiastic will be disillusioned in a very short time and the more cautious will cling to the barrier and soon be so disappointed that they may decide they are not cut out for skating at all. Being introduced to the ice by an instructor saves weeks of misery and starts off the beginner skater accurately.

To be taught to skate forward and backward correctly is most important. This means you will learn from the start to balance your weight properly on the right part of the skate so that later on, with the approach of more difficult steps, it will be much easier because you are accustomed to keeping your weight balanced on the skating foot.

I would advise the beginner first to hire a pair of skates and boots. These should be about a half-size smaller than you usually wear, fitting closely round the heel and ankle to give the maximum amount of support. Then have an instructor take you on to the ice and start you off properly. The pupil is always safe in choosing an instructor who is a member of the *International Professional Skating Association,* as all such instructors have to qualify to become members, and their charges for instruction are in accordance with their ability. Members of the Association are easily distinguishable by the badge they wear.

At the end of the session, if you have decided you would like to pursue the sport, the next move is to buy a pair of

boots and skates of your own. As there are a great variety of skates on the market it is preferable to have the advice of your instructor as to which make will suit you best. Although the skate is very important it is not as essential to have a perfect skate as a perfect boot. A few years ago I put a lot of thought and experience into designing an all purpose skate, bearing in mind the tendency of skaters to step on to the back of the tracing skate with painful results; I designed it with a short back and front which obviates this danger. I also raised the heel slightly to assist the skater in using the radius of the skate correctly. Naturally I always skate on it and think it is the best. The skate shown in Plate 1, facing page 16, is the skate I designed and is called the 'Maestro'. The boot must fit like a glove, especially round the heel and ankle, so that the heel does not slide about inside the boot. This would make it more difficult to control the edge, so it is essential the ankle should receive the maximum amount of support to enable you to keep it perfectly upright at all times. It is much better, therefore, to buy a cheaper skate than a boot of inferior quality, if you have to make a choice.

As to clothes: in the case of a girl, either a short skirt and pullover, or dress, is admirable. For a man, an ordinary suit or flannels is quite in order.

Now, as you are all set to start, the instructor will explain that the skate has two edges, the outside edge which is the one on the outside of the boot and the inside edge, the one on the inside of the boot. This may seem to be explaining the obvious but the non-skater usually looks upon a skate as

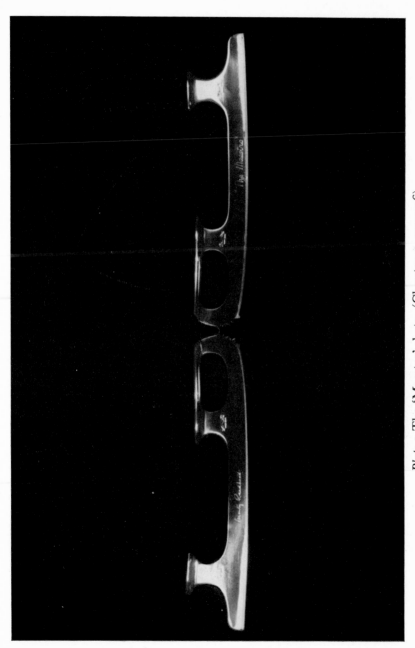

Plate 1 The 'Maestro' skate. (Chapter 1, page 16)

Plate 2 Forward skating – the wrong way. Walking forward and so not able to place the body over the left foot. (Chapter 1, page 17)

Plate 3 Forward skating – the right way. Body able to balance on top of the left foot, knee and ankle bending naturally, concertina fashion. Pushing foot is turned out to enable the push to be made with the inside edge. (Chapter 1, page 17)

a straight piece of steel upon which one balances, not knowing that it is hollow ground and thus forms two edges instead of one.

For those who cannot afford instruction I will give a brief outline of the correct procedure in forward and backward skating. The majority of beginners believe the thing to do is to lean forward and push hard. This is a mistake for it only throws the weight forward on to the front of the skate and, eventually, if one is not very careful, on to the face. The reason for this is that the skate is slightly curved and so the weight must be kept on the back of the skate to drive it forward. For the same reason the skater must be on the front of the skate when skating backwards. Leaning forward merely throws your weight on to the front of the skate and, if done to excess, on to the toe rake – with dire results! Another natural thing to do is to walk forward, pushing the skate you wish to stand on in front of you, making it quite impossible for you to do so. At this stage, if you liken the skate to a children's scooter it should give you some idea of what you are trying to do. The child stands firmly on top of the scooter and pushes backward with the other foot to propel him forward. This, in effect, is exactly what you should try to do when skating. The ice surface being slippery, if your body is propelled forward by pushing backwards against the ice with one foot, the skate you are standing on will slide forward. THE TRACING FOOT, or the FOOT YOU ARE STANDING ON SHOULD BE DIRECTLY BENEATH YOUR HIP. It follows, therefore, that for perfect balance you should NOT be able to see your tracing foot. See Plates 2 and 3, between pages 16–17.

The correct procedure is to stand perfectly erect, but not stiffly, turn out your right foot and push gently backward with the inside edge of the skate, making a short stroke with no jabbing action at the end of the stroke, for that would only upset your balance. Hold the free foot still when it

B

comes off the ice. After a slight pause, slowly straighten the tracing knee and draw the feet together, keeping your weight on the tracing foot. Make another short pause with the feet together and two feet on the ice, then repeat this action by turning out the left foot and stroking on to the right foot. (The free leg is the leg which is off the ice and the tracing leg or foot is the one on which you are standing.)

For backward skating proceed in the same manner but this time you have your weight on the front of the skate and you turn your right foot in to enable you to push against the ice with the inside edge of the skate, to propel you backward. This time the stroke is made by pushing against the ice in front of you, once more keeping your tracing foot directly beneath your hip. See Plates 4 and 5 between pages 32–33.

When you are able to skate comfortably round the rink on your own without wondering when you are going to fall, you must learn how to stop, because most accidents are caused by the inability of skaters to do so correctly.

There are many ways of stopping and the more of these you master the better, as you never know in which position you might be when required to stop. I will not go into a lengthy discussion of these positions because without practical demonstration the average beginner would not be able to understand. One very simple and effective way is for the skater to bend the tracing knee, slide the free foot in front of you, place it on the ice, turn it in and press against the ice in much the same way as you would if you were pushing backwards. Care must be taken to lean back while doing this as the tendency will be to throw you forward.

An instructor would then teach you to do edges in half circles round the rink, both forward and backward, following this with teaching you how to cross your feet, both in front and behind.

As this book is written purely from a dancing point of

view, I do not intend to go into details about the figures necessary, but just to give advice as to what you should do before attempting to dance. However, I strongly recommend you to learn to do all the edges both forward and backward, also forward outside three turns, mohawks and crossing steps reasonably well in good style and without feeling you might fall off the edge at any moment. Otherwise more than likely you will acquire bad habits which are still manifest when eventually, through a considerable amount of hard work, you have become a good dancer.

Assuming you can now do the movements, you are in a position to learn the steps of a dance. By this I mean *one* dance. You must not be impatient and try to learn all the dances at once, but to do the correct steps of one dance reasonably well before overloading the mind with the others. If you do too much at a time you will only tend to develop faults by dropping into the wrong steps where similarity occurs. There are a great number of skaters who pick up the steps of various dances here and there, resulting in a jumble which they claim to be a Foxtrot, Fourteen-step or Waltz. This type of dancer is usually very keen on exhibiting his or her skill to the beginner and is only too pleased to teach all he has himself acquired. I am not going to say that all such self-acquired knowledge is entirely wrong, but as a rule there is a lack of accuracy in such things as mohawks, placings and the crossing of the feet, either in front or behind. If you carry on steadily you will get there much quicker.

When some kindly disposed person starts you off on a new dance and tells you to put your feet together when you should cross behind, or vice-versa, such advice sticks and takes some getting rid of. You might think it absurd to suggest that it is difficult to correct original faults but when you are dancing and trying to keep a good free leg, deportment and neat footwork, it is quite natural when travelling at speed to fall into the steps you have already done. The regularity with which you make the same mistakes is quite surprising even though you may be trying hard to correct them.

Beginners who watch dancing usually admire the fast moving Fourteen-step, thinking to themselves how they would like to fly round like that and at the same time telling themselves it would be too difficult for them to attempt it for a very long time. In actual steps this is about the most simple dance, so simple that a really good Fourteen-step is seldom seen, most skaters sacrificing accuracy for speed. The beginner usually learns the Waltz first, which is really one of the most difficult dances to execute well. However, as long as the beginner is taught the right way from the start it matters little which dance he learns first.

Before giving you a description of any particular dance it would be a good thing if you were to memorise the following :

1. On no account look at your feet. Train yourself from the very start to feel what your feet are doing. Looking down is one of the easier habits to form but the most difficult to correct and one which loses a dancer many points in competition.

2. Deportment. Develop good carriage by keeping the body in an easy, upright position with the weight evenly balanced on the skating foot. Never allow yourself to bend forward from the waist. Remember that in dancing there are two people to be considered and should you bend forward, your heads become nearly touching and the lower portion of the body stands as much as two feet from the partner, giving the appearance of one propping up the other.

3. How to hold. The lady should hold her right arm firmly out at about shoulder level with the elbow slightly dropped, the left hand resting on her partner's shoulder, elbow resting lightly on the top of his. The gentleman's left arm should be held out in the same manner as the lady's right. The lady's left elbow and the man's right should be

slightly raised. Right hand is placed on the lady's back just below the left shoulder blade. As the man's hand is on the lady's back it is up to her to see that her left shoulder does not advance towards his right. This means that the lady must take care not to pull with her left hand, a slight pressure away from her being preferable. The fingers should be closed, never spread out, and the hand must not slide about but remain in the same position throughout the dance.

Be sure that the tracing knee rises and falls to the time of the music. Stiff-knee'd dancing looks wooden and lacks rhythm. Keep the free leg well turned out and the toe pointed hard down.

Now please study Plates 6, 7 and 8 facing page 33. Plate 6 illustrates bad deportment, Plate 7 shows good deportment and the correct Waltz hold, and Plate 8 is of the correct Waltz hold from the opposite side.

CHAPTER TWO

What is Dancing?

Dancing on ice. I feel a few words on this subject would be beneficial.

Firstly we have those who think the chief thing a dancer should acquire is a flowing easy movement, with the maximum amount of rhythm, combined with neatness and speed in keeping with the type of dance they are performing. I belong to this category.

Secondly, there are those who seem to think that speed is the first and foremost thing the dancer must acquire, even at the risk of becoming very untidy in attaining it, totally disregarding the fact that it is dancing they are doing and not pair skating.

Let us review the two schools of thought in their order :

First. The person who leans towards this type of dancing very soon finds out that there is more in it than he at first imagined. It requires a considerable amount of groundwork and painstaking practice to get the movements coming easily, with neatness, accuracy and good style; so he learns that if he wishes to become a really expert dancer he has to practice these movements very slowly until they become the natural thing to do. Then, and then only, is it possible for the dancer to combine speed with accuracy.

The person who follows this style of dancing usually has a strong sense of rhythm and is inclined, first, to interpret the movement characteristic to the particular dance which he and his partner are performing and, second, to let the speed come naturally as he becomes more sure of himself.

Second. A certain amount of speed in dancing is essential as long as we do not try for excessive speed at the expense of time, rhythm and character of the dance we are endeavouring to express. When this happens it is no longer dancing but a series of steps which could quite easily be done to any tune that happens to be played, without the trouble of changing the music to – say – Tango, Blues, Fourteen-step etc.

In skating, as in every other walk of life, we have the person who tries to run before he can walk. This type of person always goes for speed in an endeavour to cover up his or her lack of accuracy. It is very common to see a complete novice dash round the ice at great speed but with complete lack of control. You see, it is very simple to go fast with little practice if one is content to put technique on one side.

Having given my views on the disadvantages of speed in dancing, please do not misunderstand me and think I am against speed. On the contrary I am all for speed – combined with accuracy – providing you do not travel faster than the rhythm of the music being played. There are those who will say : How can you travel faster than the rhythm of the music if you are dancing? This is a good question and worthy of a little thought and discussion.

First of all, what is RHYTHM? How does it differ from what we know as TIME? My interpretation of rhythm is that it is a measured accent as opposed to time, which is a measure of the time of the music being played i.e. 4/4 or Foxtrot time, representing four crotchets to the bar, usually with a strong accent on the first beat and a slightly weaker one on the third beat in the bar. The accent on the first and third beats in the bar represents a simple straightforward Foxtrot rhythm. Now, if we wish to vary this rhythm, we may decide to accentuate the second and fourth beats, in fact many of our modern beat groups are doing just this or, if we wish to go further, we can break down these four crotchets into eight quavers or sixteen semi-quavers, (two quavers or four semi-quavers being equal to one crotchet). By the use of accents and rests we can produce various rhythms, for example let us take the Rhumba. Although this is 4/4 timing, or four crotchets to the bar, the rhythm is based on eight quavers to the bar, the accent usually coming in on the first, fourth and seventh quavers.

Now, to revert to the original question, I would explain it in this way. Feel the rhythm of the music and interpret it in your dancing. While you are doing this you are not conscious of the speed at which you are travelling but after a certain speed the feeling of the music is overcome by a sense of speed. That, I think, explains what I mean when I speak of travelling faster than the rhythm of the music.

A good example of this can be given by reference to the motor car, which all motorists will understand. While a car is travelling within its maximum cruising speed it purrs along in a rhythmical manner but as soon as you overdrive it you experience a feeling of suppressed excitement and it is at this point that the sense of rhythm is overcome by a sense of speed.

Some good advice I would give to all those who aspire to dance – keep uppermost in your mind the definition of dancing as given by the Encyclopaedia :

'*Dancing* – The art of performing graceful and rhythmical motions of limbs and body, usually with a musical accompaniment.'

CHAPTER THREE

The Preliminary Waltz

3/4 time – Tempo 45

This dance and the preliminary Foxtrot is primarily meant to initiate the beginner, through easy stages, to the intricacies of ice dancing. You will first be taught to hold outside edges to a count of three, both forward and backward, the free-leg being held perfectly still where it comes off the ice, with the foot turned out and the toe pointed, approximately three inches off the ice. After a count of two, slowly start straightening the tracing knee and draw the free-foot up to the tracing-foot, timing it to give a slight pause with the feet together before stroking off on to the other foot on the first beat of the next bar. When travelling forward, the heel of the pushing foot should come off the ice directly in line with the heel of the tracing-foot and be held about three inches off the ice.

Particular care must be taken not to allow the free-foot to kick up, which is a common fault and is usually caused by incorrect pushing with a strong jab of the foot against the ice at the end of the stroke. This also tends to make the skater bend forward from the waist and to get a sudden straightening of the tracing-knee, both of which are very bad faults. Likewise, when travelling backward, the heel of the pushing foot should come off the ice directly in line with the tracing-toe. See Plate 9 facing page 48.

You will be taught the open forward and backward chassé, which consists of two steps. A right or left outside edge is held for two beats then the free-foot is brought to the side of the tracing-foot and placed on the ice. The tracing-foot is then lifted slightly off the ice without moving it either forward or backward, and placed back on to the ice, after a space of one beat, exactly where it came off. See Plates 10 and 11, between pages 48–49.

Care must be taken when lifting the foot off the ice that it is not lifted too high – about an inch is plenty. Too often we see the foot lifted clumsily about five or six inches in the air. If you were to ask one of these skaters why they lifted their skate so high they would probably tell you they were doing it to show they were not double-tracking. Double-tracking is travelling with two feet on the ice at the same time, with both skates travelling in the same direction; this is not allowed in a skating test. Although you are not allowed to double-track, the movement should be done very neatly with the foot being lifted just slightly off the ice. Otherwise it interferes with the flowing action of the dance and often leads to dancing out of time. Before being taught the Preliminary Waltz, you will have been shown how to turn a forward outside three-turn on both feet. In this dance, however, only the left three-turn is used, which is rather unfortunate because it tends to encourage the skater to practise the left three more than the right. This is a bad thing because later when you learn the European Waltz you will be required to turn threes equally well on either foot. To the beginner skater, therefore, let me say right at the start that whatever you practice make sure you practice the movement on both feet.

Talking about both feet, most skaters feel stronger on one foot than the other. The logical thing to do is to practise the weaker foot more than the stronger, but the more natural thing is to skate mostly the things we like or find easier to do. If, then, you wish to become a good skater acquire the habit of practising your weaker movements first. You notice I say weaker movements, not weak foot. I say this because weakness does not confine itself to the feet. You may be left-handed and you will naturally pick things up or do what you wish to do with your left, just as a right-handed person will use the right. This does not only apply to the feet. Most people have a preference for moving in either a clockwise or anti-clockwise direction. The majority of skaters tend to prefer the anti-clockwise rotation movement. This, of course, is accentuated by the fact that very few, if any, of our rinks these days have any periods where the skaters have to skate the reverse or clockwise way round the rink.

This is, of course, an instructional book, and my aim is to make it as easy as possible for the lady or man to turn its pages and sort out what they want to know as quickly as possible. However, where necessary for clarity or where I feel a point wants pressing home, I shall deliberately repeat myself. I am mentioning this now because I am about to link together the above steps to form the Waltz movement. I shall commence with the lady, and as this is the first effort at dancing I shall follow on with a rather full description of the gentleman's steps, even though there is basically no difference other than they commence backwards for the lady and forwards for the gentleman. However, my long experience as a teacher has taught me never to take it for granted that the pupil will understand. It is very clear to the teacher but often like a foreign language to the pupil.

Lady: In linking these steps together, let us start by explaining that the dance is performed in the Waltz hold, and in order to perform the dance together we have first to arrive at the Waltz hold. For this we do a series of steps devised to bring the partners into the dancing position. Although the steps are optional, the following is normal. Standing in hand-in-hand hold, strike gently on to the left foot, following this with another on to the right foot. Then make a third stroke on to the left forward outside edge, slowly draw your feet together and turn a three-turn. This will bring you opposite your partner and directly in front. Place your right foot on to the ice close to the side of the left foot on to a right back outside edge.

You are now in the position to start the dance, having taken four steps to get there. The first step is a chassé commencing on a left back outside edge which is held for two beats. The right foot is placed on the ice, close to the tracing foot, on to a right back inside edge and the tracing foot is lifted slightly off the ice, just about an inch, neither moving forward or backward of the new tracing foot. This is held for one beat, after which the left foot is replaced by the side of the right foot on a left back outside edge and held for three beats with the free leg carried in front – the free leg turned out and the toe pointed. These three steps should have formed a semi-circle in a clockwise direction. The movement is now repeated precisely but with the curve moving in an anti-clockwise direction.

To do this we stroke on to a right back outside edge, held for two beats, the left foot then being placed on a back inside for one beat – this of course being a right foot chassé as opposed to the previous one which was the left foot chassé. The right foot is then replaced on a right back outside edge and held for three beats. These two chassés have to be performed a minimum of twice and a maximum of four times after which the lady steps forward on to a left forward outside edge which is held for three beats. This is followed by a forward chassé in a clockwise direction, the edges being right forward outside 2 beats, left forward inside 1 beat, right forward outside 3 beats.

We now come to the anti-clockwise chassé, left forward outside 2 beats, right forward inside 1 beat, left forward outside 3 beats. As with the backward movement you may skate a minimum of two and a maximum of four chassés. It may be as well here to explain that the chassé consists of two edges, the first being the 2 beat and the second the 1 beat, the following edge, the 3 beat, is the linking edge between the chassés.

The dancers having decided whether they will skate two

or four chassés, the lady proceeds as follows: after either the second or fourth chassé the lady will skate the left forward outside edge as though she were going to repeat the sequence but will slowly straighten the tracing knee; at the same time she slowly draws the free foot up to the tracing foot so that the big toe joint of the free foot fits snugly into the hollow of the tracing foot, just below the instep, but does not place the skate on the ice. See Plate 12 between pages 64–65. This movement should be performed so that it will take precisely two beats, because on the third beat in the bar she will turn a three turn and hold that back inside edge for the remaining beat, after which she will place a right back outside edge close beside the left foot and hold the edge for three beats. Those are the steps of the Preliminary Waltz and they are repeated in this order until the end of the music.

Gentleman: As I have explained to the lady, the dance is performed in the Waltz hold and in order to get into the Waltz hold a series of steps are devised to bring this about. Standing in hand-in-hand hold, strike gently on to the left foot, following this with another on the right foot. You then make a third stroke on to the left forward outside edge, slowly draw your feet together and place your right forward inside edge on to the ice close by the side of the tracing foot – on the third beat in the bar lifting the tracing foot slightly off the ice and holding it for one beat. This is known as a chassé and in this instance is used as a timing step whilst the lady turns a three turn. She will now be facing you and as she, on the first beat of the next bar, strikes on to right back outside, you strike on to left forward outside directly in front of her, taking up the Waltz hold. This edge is held for three beats.

You are now ready to commence the dance, the steps of which are as follows: Right forward outside edge – 2 beats. Slowly straighten your tracing knee, draw your feet together and place your left foot close beside the right on to a left

forward inside edge. At the same time lift the right foot
slightly off the ice approximately one inch, taking care that
the right foot does not move either forward or backward of
the tracing foot. This edge is held for one beat, the two edges
forming what is known as a forward chassé. It is followed
by a right forward outside edge and held for three beats.
This movement forms a semi-circle in a clockwise direction
and is followed by a similar movement in an anti-clockwise
direction, consisting of left forward outside edge held for two
beats, after which the right foot is brought up to the left and
placed by its side on a right forward inside edge, one beat.
Then comes left forward outside edge, three beats.

I must tell you at this stage that the dancers may choose
to do either two or four forward or backward chassés. Should
they decide on four, then the three-beat left forward outside
edge is held for the full three beats and the sequence repeated,
but at the end of the fourth chassé the gentleman must turn
a three turn to take him round to backwards. This is done
by striking on to the left forward outside edge as though you
are going to repeat but instead you slowly straighten the
tracing knee and at the same time slowly draw the free foot
up to the tracing foot by the instep, keeping the heel down.
The skate must, however, not touch the ice. This movement
must take precisely two beats of music, for on the third beat
in the bar you have to turn a three and hold the back inside
edge for the remaining one beat – this is of course assuming
the turn takes no measureable time to perform. After holding
the inside edge for one beat you place the right foot close
beside the left foot and strike on to a right back outside edge
which will be held for three beats.

You now proceed to skate two or four chassés backwards,
which are performed in a similar manner to those you have
skated forward, the edges being as follows : left back outside,
2 beats, right back inside, 1 beat, left back outside, 3 beats,
forming the clockwise curve. Right back outside, 2 beats, left

back inside, 1 beat, right back outside, 3 beats. Whether you are doing two or four chassés this edge is held for its full three beats, slowly bringing your feet together on the third beat in the bar so that your free leg does not impede the lady who will be turning her left forward three. On the first beat of the next bar you strike forward on to a left forward outside edge directly towards your partner, this edge being held for three beats.

That completes the sequence of steps of the Preliminary Waltz, from here onwards it is repetition until the music stops playing.

Dancing the Preliminary Waltz together

You are both fully familiar with your own steps and now the big moment comes when you learn how to skate them with a partner. It would be wrong if I did not mention here that the object of both dancers is to move in such a manner that the combined effort will blend so well that neither stands out but the whole moves as one person. This is, of course, the ideal and will not be achieved for some considerable time; however, if you ever wish to dance in this delightful manner, from the very beginning you must keep the ideal uppermost in your mind. I will endeavour to help you to do just this in the pages that follow.

Before we can dance together we have to find a comfortable way of arriving in the Waltz hold. The steps we use for doing so are completely optional, the rule being that we may use up to seven steps of our own choice. The dancers should, however, avoid being too showy. The best way is usually the easy way.

If we take the first four steps I described for the lady and the first four for the gentleman and start by holding the hand-in-hand hold, we shall arrive in the Waltz hold. The first two edges may be either outsides or insides but I prefer to skate them in the following way : left forward inside, right forward outside. The lady now strikes left forward outside and turns a three on the third beat, the man striking his left forward outside directly in line with the lady, doing a chassé by bringing his feet together on the count of three as the lady makes her turn. At the completion of the turn the partners will be facing one another.

All that remains now is to take up the correct hold which is as follows; and may be checked by reference to Plates 6, 7 and 8 facing page 33.

The hold: Facing each other the man places his right hand on the lady's back so that his right hand will be resting on her left shoulder blade. I mention this rather obvious placing of the man's right hand because it is not uncommon to see the hand either too far across the lady's back, under her arm or even down the small of her back! The lady's left arm should rest on the man's right, with her elbow immediately above her partner's, both their elbows being slightly raised. The lady's right and the man's left arms are extended at approximately shoulder height with the elbows slightly dropped. So much for the actual hold, but we must bear in mind that the position of the bodies must also be taken into account. It is not uncommon to see a couple dancing the Waltz who, although they may be facing one another, are slightly 'off square' with one another as illustrated by the photograph. 'Alignment of shoulders'. (Plate 13, between pages 64–65). The lady's left and the man's right shoulder and hip should be directly opposite, the shoulders and hips forming a square. They should remain like this throughout the dance.

Plate 4 Backward skating – the wrong way. Not turning the foot in for the backward push; the pushing foot slides forward and there is no grip on the ice. (Chapter 1, page 18)

Plate 5 Backward skating – the right way. The pushing foot is turned in, allowing the inside edge to bite into the ice for the skater to push against. (Chapter 1, page 18)

Plate 6 RIGHT: Bad deportment. Bent forward, from the hips, heads down, shoulders rolled forward, arms bent, free leg not turned out or toe pointed, fingers spread. (Chapter 1, page 21) *Plate* 7 BOTTOM LEFT: Good deportment and the correct Waltz hold. Body and head erect, no bending at the hips. Lady's right arm and man's left extended with elbows slightly dropped. Free leg turned out and toe pointed. (Chapter 1, page 21). *Plate* 8 BOTTOM RIGHT: Correct Waltz hold, taken from the opposite side to show Lady's left elbow resting on man's right. Free legs turned out and toes pointed. (Chapter 1, page 21)

CHAPTER FOUR

The Foxtrot Movement

(better known as the Preliminary Foxtrot)
Tempo 4/4 at 26 b.p.m.

This movement forms the second part of the Preliminary Bronze Dance Test and although it is very simple in its conception – 'consisting only of a run to the left followed by a 4 beat left edge with swing, the same being repeated to the right' – to perform it really well is far from simple.

What is not generally realised is that a running movement on ice requires a considerable amount of skilful manipulation of the pushing foot. If we are to do as stated – run – then this must be done with the same freedom of movement as when running off the ice. On a slippery surface, this is easier said than done and, in fact, is rarely seen as a true running action although it can be performed so beautifully and is really a treat to watch. I have always said that running on ice is a Gold movement.

You will be asking why the Preliminary Foxtrot, which is one of the first dancing movements we learn, should consist of running steps when I say that they are so difficult to perform? The answer is that whilst the running movement requires considerable skill to do really well, it is one of the first movements which will be picked up by the beginner. If picked up wrongly, which is more than likely, it will take perseverance, concentration and hard work to correct and perfect should you, at some later date, aspire to first class dancing.

If the teacher, from the very beginning, insists on the correct technique for running, and even if the pupil is, at this stage, unable to do the movement correctly, he will eventually arrive at his goal. Incidentally, it is very rarely that we see correct running in a Preliminary Bronze Dance Test – some licence obviously being allowed by the Judges. More often than not I have noticed the Preliminary Foxtrot being danced by a series of crossing steps as opposed to running steps. There are many who think you do cross over when running on the ice; indeed, when we look at a person running correctly, there does appear to be a crossing movement, until we look more closely. This is due to the action of the feet, which have to turn to enable us to get a grip of the ice with the pushing foot. I shall now give a description of the action of the pushing foot and free leg whilst running. Please refer to Plate 14 facing page 65.

Running on ice

I shall describe this fully in an anti-clockwise direction and briefly in a clockwise direction, the movement being exactly the same but using the opposite edges.

A run may consist of any multiple of two edges, though in a dance it is rare for it to consist of more than two.

Striking normally on to a left forward outside edge, turning out the right foot so as to push with the inside edge. So far it is the same as an ordinary skating stroke but at this stage the action changes. In a normal stroke the pushing foot at the completion of the stroke would remain quite still, held behind the tracing foot, with the foot turned out and the toe pointed. As there is no pause in a running movement, immediately the right foot completes its stroke it is moving straight forward to brush past the tracing foot and on to the ice. Immediately the right foot starts moving, the left foot, whilst maintaining the outside edge, starts turning in to push backward with the outside edge. The pivot of the pushing foot is made on the front of the skate so that the toe of the pushing foot remains over the line of travel and the heel comes away from it to allow free passage of the right foot. The turning in of the left foot to push with the outside edge is what makes it appear that the right is crossing over the left. Given a moment's thought it is not difficult to realise that it is impossible to run with feet crossing, whether we are on or off the ice. The steps and the movement are exactly the same for the lady and gentleman and I will, therefore, describe them together.

Lady's and Gentleman's Steps

	BEATS		COUNT
Left forward outside ⎫	I	run	I
Right forward inside ⎭	I		2
Left forward outside	4	swing	3, 4, I, 2
Right forward outside ⎫	I	run	3
Left forward inside ⎭	I		4
Right forward outside	4	swing	I, 2, 3, 4

You will observe that there are only six steps in this dance and therefore it is not likely to tax your memory very much to remember them. This is a good thing because it will allow you to concentrate fully on accuracy of footwork, movement, timing and good carriage or deportment. When mentioning carriage we are usually referring to the body being held erect with the head up. If we say deportment, it is true that it means the same thing. Why, then, bother to use the word carriage at all? The reason is that when we are dancing on the ice the free leg has to be carried off the ice, either quite still or moving forward or backward for periods of two, four or more beats of music. Therefore, to enhance the general appearance the free leg is carried with the foot turned out and the toe pointed. I cannot stress too strongly the importance of the carriage of the free leg in completing the picture we produce when dancing with good deportment. In view of this I feel that carriage is probably the better word as applied to ice.

Referring to the list of steps, you will observe that they consist of a two edge run to the left, left forward outside –

right forward inside, followed by a four beat left forward outside. The same movement is then repeated to the right – right forward outside – left forward inside, followed by a four beat right forward outside edge. You will also notice that I have given figures under the heading 'count'. You may say this is pretty obvious but you must realise that there are many people who do not find timing easy. For these counting is a must, particularly in this dance because you see that after the run the four beat edge starts on the third beat of the bar and carries over the bar to the third beat of the next bar, which means the run to the right starts on the third beat with the four beat edge starting on the first beat in the bar and lasting until the first beat of the next bar, when the whole is repeated. I find with bad timekeepers that skating the first four beat edge – left forward outside – starting on the third beat and carrying over the bar causes some confusion, particularly as the next four beat edge starts at the beginning of the bar and ends at the beginning of the next.

Many dancers who have difficulty in keeping time to the music think that when they say 'four' they have done four beats when in fact a beat lasts from beat to beat and is not complete until the beginning of the next beat. To illustrate this I have drawn two bars of music:

As you will see, you place your foot on to the ice on a particular beat, shown figure-wise, and the connecting line shows how it runs on to the next beat before being complete: i.e. when a child is born we don't say he is one until he has lived exactly a year. Music is the same; we place our foot on to the ice as the beat begins but that beat is not complete until it arrives at the next beat.

CHAPTER FIVE

The Preliminary Bronze Dance Test

The test consists of the Waltz Movement and the Foxtrot Movement. In order to obtain your Preliminary Bronze Medal you have to make application to the National Skating Association of Great Britain on the approved test form as supplied by the N.S.A. These forms are obtainable at any ice rink either from the Secretary of the Dance Club or from the office. You will be required to become a member of the N.S.A. and will have to pay a small judging fee. You will find full details on the back of the form. I mention all this because when we let a person apply for their first test the questions always are: 'How do I apply?' 'Where do I get the test papers?' 'How do I fill them in?'

On the paper you will be asked where you would like the test to take place, and when – at least fourteen days notice being required. This is necessary to allow for arranging the judges. It does not necessarily mean you will get your test in fourteen days but you should be prepared to take it should it come up. In the busy part of the season there is sometimes quite a wait.

A point I would like to mention is that the N.S.A. are not under any obligation to give you your test at the rink you request, although they usually endeavour to do so.

It is common practice these days for the pupil to keep asking: 'When can I go in for my medal test?' Why not wait until your teacher tells you. He is just as keen as you are that you should take your test as soon as you are ready. If you leave it to your teacher you will go in for your test with confidence, knowing that you are really up to the standard, no doubt thereby saving yourself the all too common failure through trying to skip the basic.

Should you, through being blessed with a natural rhythm and movement, manage to pass your test though somewhat weak in technique, this could well jeopardise your future. This is because it is most difficult for a pupil to revise the basic technique again should he or she later desire to go on to the top. It has happened in the past, and no doubt will happen again, that potentially top class dancers show this weakness even when skating in championships.

The judges will, in the main, be looking for the following features :

(a) First and foremost, movement in perfect time with the music. If you are out of time you are just not dancing and there is nothing to judge.

(b) Secondly, correct striking or pushing. That is to say, pushing with the edge of the skate and not the toe – the latter not on any account being allowed.

(c) Thirdly, good deportment and carriage of the free leg. Correct hold.

(d) Last but not least, movement – i.e. graceful and rhythmical movement in unison with the music and blending in with that of the partner. One very important thing in this respect is what is known as rise and fall, meaning the bending and straightening of the tracing knee.

CHAPTER SIX

The British Fourteen-Step
Tempo 56 – 2/4 or 6/8

Although this dance is often referred to as the Tenstep, there are actually fourteen steps in it. Originally there were only ten but as this dance is performed in a circle, the first chassé is now repeated in order to make a larger circle. The extra chassé is also a great help in gaining speed. Until a few years ago the tempo was set at 6/8 or march time, but it is now optional whether 6/8 or 2/4 tempo is played. This makes little difference, for both have an exhilarating beat which causes most people to fall into the spirit of the music with complete abandon, frequently totally disregarding style, footwork and often time. The partners merely pull one another round, their movements getting more and more untidy as the dance progresses. It is amazing sometimes how they manage to keep on their skates. The main cause of this is the inability of the dancers to do mohawks properly on their own. It is a great pity this dance is not given the attention it deserves because when it is done properly it is most enjoyable and rhythmical.

The British Fourteen-step is danced in the Waltz hold. Unlike the Waltz, the footwork is different in places. In the beginning the lady does crossed chassés while the man does open chassés; the lady has to do an outside open mohawk whilst the man does an inside open mohawk. In view of these differences I shall describe the lady's and gentleman's steps separately.

The lady's first edge is right back outside, placed on to the ice close to the inside of the left foot and is followed by left back inside crossed in front. Particular care must be taken here as it is a common fault for the lady to cross the foot over very wide, causing her body to move over to the right. This will bring her body out of line with her partner and initiate the next fault, placing step No. 3, right back outside, also wide – thus making steps 1, 2 and 3 very untidy and somewhat unbalanced.

A very attractive movement in this dance is step No. 4, left back outside. This is the only breakaway from the circle and if done with a nice swaying action is pleasant to skate and to watch. However, if the first three steps have been done with wide footwork and the body falling into the circle, it is unlikely that the dancer will manage to skate a left back outside at all but will skate left back inside. This will make it impossible for the man to skate his corresponding right forward outside edge.

Steps 5, 6 and 7 are indentical to the first three and to add emphasis I will repeat them : Step No. 1, right back outside placed close to the inside of the left foot. No. 2, crossed neatly over the front and placed close to the outside of the right foot. No. 3, placed close to the inside of the left foot.

To the lady who tries to dance before she is ready or has the bad habit of leaning forward from the waist, the crossing step provides another stumbling block. When she leans forward it causes the free leg to come in contact with the ice before it is up to the tracing foot, making a very inelegant step and causing her to place it down out of time. It is very easy to do this step providing one stands upright and keeps the weight evenly balanced on the tracing foot. Care should also be taken on the back crossing steps not to pull into the centre, which makes the circle distorted and, in the case of the lady's seventh step, making it extremely difficult for her to get forward on the left forward outside edge in the right position. The lady must come forward on the correct edge, left forward outside, with the right shoulder and hip back, otherwise she cannot easily cross the ninth step, right forward inside, behind the left forward outside edge.

Particular care must be taken on the seventh step not to rotate the body. As the right back outside is placed on to the ice, the left foot comes off in front and the heel is brought back approximately to the ankle of the tracing foot ready to strike on to left forward outside. The body should then naturally revolve with the man as he does his inside mohawk.

On steps 10, 11, 12 and 13 the lady often pulls away from her partner and tries to run into the circle, which makes it almost impossible for her to do the right edges and usually leads up to a very bad mohawk because the hips and shoulders will automatically come into the wrong position. There must not be any pulling either into or out of the circle. Each edge must follow on in the same line as the previous one, with her body facing out of the circle, hips and shoulders parallel to her partner's.

The lady's mohawk, steps 12 and 13, should be done with the right side pressed back and keeping the body weight, while skating the first part, left forward outside, as far as is possible over the right leg and therefore making it easy to reach the ice when placing the right back outside on to the ice. This being an open mohawk, step 13, right back outside should be placed on to the ice to the inside of the left foot, approximately by the instep, with the foot turned out as far as possible. When placing the right foot on the ice, place the ball of the foot on to the ice and run the left foot off, keeping it turned out so that it comes off directly in line and behind the new tracing foot, right back outside. The last step, left back inside, is placed in the hollow of the right foot.

The general faults for the lady are bending forward, placing the feet down wide apart, pulling into the circle and therefore causing general distortion of the dance and in particular the outside edges of the mohawk skated on insides.

In dancing you should never have two feet on the ice together – this is called double-tracking – but I must mention that lack of knowledge of what double-tracking really is causes some very ugly movements. For instance, when making the push it is necessary to have both feet on the ice in order to have something to push against. A good parallel for this can be found in the children's scooter. The skate very much resembles this. Like the scooter it is just to stand on whilst the body is pushed along. If the child were to lift the scooter off the ground he could not push it along. Some skaters try to push and get the skate off the ice at the same time, causing the body to lurch forward with a subsequent loss of power. Two feet, therefore, must be on the ice while pushing. This is *not* double-tracking. Double-tracking is when two feet are running parallel to one another in the same direction. Likewise, in order to perform a mohawk smoothly, it is necessary to perform it on two feet, although you would be double-tracking were you to keep the left foot on the ice after the mohawk is completed.

Although there is a glossary of dance terms at the end of the book, there are certain things the pupil has to have constantly brought to his notice. I shall therefore draw your attention to the fact that the mohawk in this dance for both the lady and the man are open mohawks. The new skating foot is placed on the ice to the inside of the tracing foot which in turn comes off the ice behind the new tracing foot. Should you place the foot to the outside of the tracing foot and bring the free foot off in front, it would become a closed mohawk and you would be doing the dance incorrectly.

I have already mentioned double-tracking; there is a strong tendency for the lady to do this on her back crossing steps, but in this dance double-tracking by the man seems to be more usual. The majority of men forget to lift their left skate off the ice when doing the second edge of the chassé and just slide it along.

The man's Fourteen-step commences with a left forward

outside edge placed close to the inside of the right foot. Steps
1 and 2 form the chassé, great care being taken when placing
the right forward inside edge close beside the left foot that it
does not pass the left foot before placing. The next part of
the chassé is to lift the left foot a short distance off the ice
(approximately one inch) care also being taken that it does
not slip forward. It is lifted straight up and placed down
again by the side of the right foot on to left forward outside,
step 3. Step 4, right forward outside, must be placed by the
side of the left foot and skated with a bold outside curve to
form the only breakaway from the circle in the dance, coin-
ciding with the lady's 4th step, left back outside and both
bodies swaying outwards and then back to the circle on the
next edge. Steps 5, 6 and 7 are a repeat of 1, 2 and 3.

On the man's eighth and ninth edges (mohawk) it is quite
common to see a 'spread eagle' turn done. The difference
being that with the spread eagle both feet are kept on the
ice with the rear foot following along the same tracing as the
forward foot and directly behind it. As this, like the lady's is
an open mohawk, the new tracing foot should be placed to
the inside of the right forward inside (step 8), and as the
left foot, left back inside (step 9), is placed on the ice, the
right foot is run off the ice behind you. While doing the
mohawk keep the weight as near as possible over the left foot
and place the front of the skate on to the ice approximately
by the instep.

After the man's mohawk the tenth edge, right back outside, should be placed neatly by the side. Steps 11, left back
inside, and 12, right back outside, are running steps and
correspond with the lady's forward movement. Care must be
taken when running that the free foot passes the skating foot
before going on to the ice. It seems to be a great temptation
on the back steps, 10, 11 and 12, for the man to slide one
foot past the other instead of making each step cleanly,
simultaneously lifting the other off. The 13th step, left back

inside, should be crossed in front and placed close to the outside of the right foot; this is important because should it be placed wide it will force the lady into the circle and make it difficult for her to do her mohawk. Another fault often displayed by the man while skating the 13th edge, even though he may have placed this correctly on to the inside edge, is to rotate his body prematurely, ready for stepping forward. This causes him to change the edge and run out of the circle pulling the lady with him and, of course, making her do a backward inside edge for the second edge of her mohawk.

The 14th edge has a number of pitfalls both for lady and gentleman; the lady often strikes vigorously on to the edge causing it to be pushed on to an outside edge and to run out of the circle, so making it impossible for the man to strike right forward inside and causing general distortion of the body positions. When striking on to the 14th edge a

The Fourteen-Step (British)

	LADY'S STEPS				MAN'S STEPS	
Edges	*Beats*		*Step No.*	*Edges*	*Beats*	
RBO	1		1	LFO	1	
LBI	1	Cross-in-front	2	RFI	1	Chassé
RBO	2		3	LFO	2	
LBO	2		4	RFO	2	
RBO	1		5	LFO	1	
LBI	1	Cross-in-front	6	RFI	1	Chassé
RBO	2		7	LFO	2	
LFO	1		8	RFI	1	Open Mohawk to
RFI	1	Cross behind	9	LBI	1	
LFO	1	Run	10	RBO	1	
RFI	1	Run	11	LBI	1	Run
LFO	1	Open Mohawk	12	RBO	1	
RBO	1		13	LBI	1	Cross-in-front
LBI	2		14	RFI	2	

minimum of body movement should be observed. Likewise, if the man does not strike forward in the right direction he can make it impossible for his partner to place correctly. Should he step wide – that is, to the left of his partner – she will have to bend forward in a most ungainly manner.

CHAPTER SEVEN

The European Waltz

Tempo 45 – 3/4

Although the Waltz is the simplest dance in actual steps, it is generally agreed that, by reason of its sheer simplicity, it has become the most difficult dance to perform in a perfectly timed, flowing, rhythmical manner.

It will therefore be obvious that this dance must be performed with a maximum amount of good style, deportment, neatness of footwork and rhythm.

Bad deportment seems to be more common in the Waltz than in any other dance. A possible reason for this is the general impression that the dance should be done so that you first face one barrier and then the other. Although this, in a sense, is quite right, it is liable to make the beginner exaggerate in his endeavour to achieve this. Consequently the partners hang on to one another and just swing round. The result is that instead of facing the barrier they are almost facing back in the direction from which they have come and have to give an energetic heave to get on to the other edge. The direction of the Waltz is first to one barrier and then to the other but do not make the mistake of rotating too far round. Should you do so, this will cause you to come back on your tracks and result in distortion of the pattern, as shown in the diagram, (wrong way) instead of as also shown (right) with the two linking edges proceeding along the transverse or short axis (See Fig. 1). The result of this error being made is a terrific heave on either side, making the partners bend forward at the waist and giving the unsatisfactory impression that they are propping each other up.

Another reason for bad deportment in this dance is the

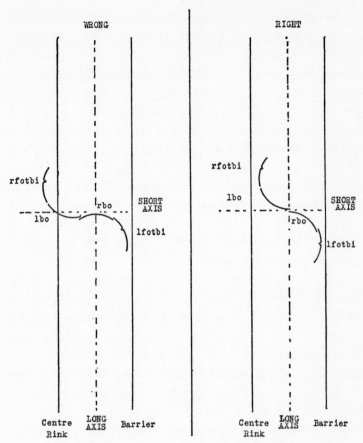

FIG 1 : *Coming back on your tracks – Waltz*

inability of the dancers to skate outside edges. When this is the case they force flats round with their bodies, try to get assistance by pulling on their partner and generally using brute force, whereas a skate placed on a true edge will go round freely and easily without any force at all.

The edges should be skated strongly but with perfect control. By control I do not mean that the dancers must be stiff and machine-like; on the contrary they should be perfectly relaxed to enable them to produce body rhythm into their dancing. All movements should be done with ease and grace; all steps should be struck from the heel; striking must be simultaneous with no sign of toe-pushing, and movements must be smooth and flowing. The three turns must not be jumped and must be cleanly performed, particular care being taken to hold the back inside edge after the turn for one beat. Probably the most common fault in the Waltz is for the three turn to be made and back outside edge placed down almost together. You must remember that, while you are holding the back inside edge after the three turn for one beat, your partner is on a back outside edge and therefore although you are facing one another, you are both travelling backwards. Whilst doing so the bodies are both revolving, which enables the person travelling on the back outside edge to strike easily forward directly in front of the partner.

On no account should the dancer try to get round his partner. Throughout the dance, the shoulders should remain level and parallel to your partner's, the two bodies revolving in perfect unison. It is quite common to see couples striking to the outside of their partner in an attempt to get round the other side. As it is impossible to get round your partner, due to the hold, the result is that the bodies are pulled out of alignment, the edges distorted and usually the three turn made on the second beat of the bar instead of the third, making the dancers hopelessly out of time. The three turn should be made directly in front of your partner, or as we know it, between your partner's feet, allowing both bodies to revolve in time with the music. The back outside edge following the three turn should be placed easily and neatly by the side of the tracing foot.

To apply rhythm it is essential for the movements to be in unison. The rise and fall of the knee, the moving of the free leg and rotation of the body all being in accordance with the time of the music and the speed at which you are travelling. The faster you travel the longer will be your edge and the knee will require more bend. It is an asset to be able to

Plate 9 Carriage of free leg in front and behind. Free heel in line
with the tracing heel when free leg is behind. Heel in line with
toe when free leg is in front. (Chapter 3, page 25)

Plate 10 Foot lifted too high in a chassé. Note the ugly position when the foot is lifted too high. (Chapter 3, page 26)

Plate 11 Chassé correctly done. (Chapter 3, page 26)

dance reasonably fast but not at the expense of good style, movement and accuracy.

I have just mentioned rise and fall and extra knee bend when travelling faster. How is the rise and fall and extra knee bend attained? The answer is simply this – by correct pushing. This sounds very easy but if you were unfortunate enough to have been allowed to do more advanced movements before you had thoroughly mastered forward and backward skating, it is more than likely you will be rocking from one foot to the other, your body weight changing as you attempt to bring your feet together. The result will be that you will push on to an already bent knee, making it impossible to rise and fall. This rise and fall is attained by placing the new skating foot on to the ice with the knee straight. The pushing foot starts to turn for the push and both start bending and continue to do so throughout the push, making a gradual transition of weight from one foot to the other. As you bring your feet together to make the next stroke your tracing knee slowly straightens in time with the music, making a smooth, flowing and graceful action which is a delight to watch. If you are doing all this correctly, the extra knee bend required for extra speed will come automatically through the extra length of stroke made to produce the extra speed.

I must add that speed should never be attempted until a dancer is quite sure of his movements, otherwise the footwork becomes untidy.

The following are one or two points which cause the beginner a considerable amount of trouble :

It is very common for the lady, when going backwards, to allow her free leg to swing back past the tracing leg. This has one or two bad effects on the dance. It causes her to be late placing her skate on the ice for the next edge and this puts her out of time with the music. It also has the effect of swinging the back edge round too sharply, causing her to pull

D

badly away from her partner which usually makes both dancers bend forward in an effort to reach one another. When this happens on the edge prior to striking forward, it makes it extremely difficult to strike. This also applies to the man.

Another fault which is common to both is this; in an endeavour to get a strong forward edge they FORCE the edge causing the hip to protrude into the circle (See Plate 15 facing page 65). This makes it almost impossible to turn the three and certainly impossible to turn a smooth one.

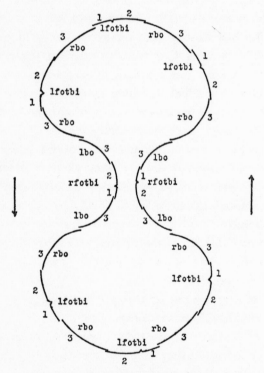

FIG 2 : *Waltz – Lady's steps*

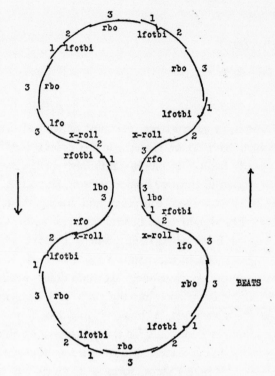

FIG 3 : *Waltz – Man's steps*

CHAPTER EIGHT

The Foxtrot

Tempo 26 – 4/4

The Foxtrot is, in actual steps, the most difficult of the three dances which have to be skated for the Bronze medal test. It offers many stumbling blocks – a number of the steps being either crossed in front or behind, or run. Beginners, therefore, often find it rather confusing and frequently cross in front when they should cross behind and *vice-versa*. Crossed steps are not difficult when done properly but are extremely so when approached in the wrong way. You quite often see the less studious or untrained dancers doing their own version of the dance, choosing the path of least resistance and doing the steps open. Although it might be much easier for them, it makes it difficult for the partner to do the right steps, the dance being arranged in such a way that the lady's steps fit into the man's steps, forming a design on the ice which the open steps would prevent them from performing. As it has become so popular among dancers to go in for medals, it is a great pity when they are asked to dance by someone who does not do the right steps. They have enough to think about in their own dancing without having to wonder what their partner is going to do next, especially if it happens to be the Bronze medal test for which they are training. As this is the first stage in their dancing career they do not have the control of the more advanced dancer.

In reviewing this dance it is necessary to start looking for trouble at the very beginning. To find out why a certain step will not go right it is often necessary to go back five or six steps and, by starting with the first steps and working up, you will be able to check your positions from the start.

Although this dance is listed by the N.S.A. of Great

Britain and the world governing body, the International Skating Union, as a preferred pattern dance, in the normal size of rink the dancer will find it beneficial in many ways to use the pattern shown in Fig 5, page 58. I will discuss this with you but first, though a short description of the preferred pattern dance is given in the Glossary of Terms on page 140, a little further explanation would be helpful at this stage. Preferred pattern means you are at liberty to start the dance and skate the edges, mohawk etc., at any part of the rink you wish but you must ensure you are able adequately to use the ice surface and at the same time be able to repeat the dance from the same place after having completed one sequence. This is, of course, providing the steps of the dance are sufficient in number to complete a whole circuit of the rink. The dance we are discussing uses only half a circuit and therefore the repeat would commence in exactly the same place on the opposite side of the rink, and at the end of the second sequence we will be back at the original starting point. This is one of the reasons why the diagram shown is preferable – it allows the edges to be skated in a flowing manner without any forcing whatsoever. Some of the other patterns you see danced often lead the dancer unwittingly to skate the wrong edges. When this happens in a test they are heavily marked down and often fail because they are not doing the dance technically correct. In teaching you the Foxtrot, therefore, I shall do so using the pattern as shown by the diagram as though it were a set pattern dance.

As the first three edges (left forward outside, right forward inside, left forward outside) curve to the left or anti-clockwise, it is advantageous to strike the first left forward outside a little towards the barrier, otherwise it will be found that on the average rink there will be insufficient space to do these edges without protruding over the centre, unless you skate these edges very weakly or come back on your track. This, perhaps, calls for a little explanation : I must mention here that a line drawn along the length of the rink between the barrier and the centre of the ice surface is known as the long axis. A line drawn at right angles to the barrier across the rink is known as the short axis. A great deal more will be said about the axes in the advanced dancing, particularly the short axis, but it would only confuse you to say any more at the moment.

When three edges are skated on the same curve it is necessary, in order to keep the dance progressive, to manoeuvre the edges so that they do not form too much of a circle and come back on their track. Coming back on your track means curving round towards the point where the long and short axes cross one another, and continuing the curve so that it crosses the short axis and goes back into the circle. For example:

Step 4, for the lady and 4a for the man, right forward outside cross-roll proceeds in the same line as the previous edge and will go over the centre line of the rink if steps 1, 2 and 3 have come back on track.

Step 4, for the lady – 4 – beat right forward outside edge – matches up with the man's 4a, right forward outside three turn to right back inside (2 beats) and 4b, left back outside edge (2 beats). The combined edges of the lady and the man, taking 4 beats in all, should gradually bring them back to the barrier. Care should be taken by the lady to follow the man's line of travel and not pull the edge round too sharply as it would make it very difficult for the man to turn his three and will, after he has made his turn, cause the lady to be on the left of the man instead of directly in front of him – which will completely upset the run of the dance. This will cause the same trouble as on steps 1, 2 and 3, the lady then finding it difficult to cross-roll for her 5th edge, left forward outside three turn.

The man must take care that his edge 4b, follows in the same line of travel as his previous edge and that he does not

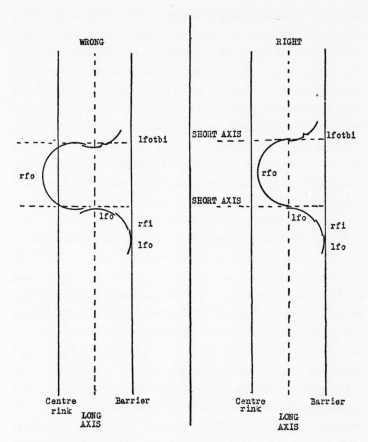

FIG 4 : *Coming back on your tracks – Foxtrot steps* 1, 2, 3, 4, 5

pull it round. Allow the edge to go round naturally. Considerable trouble is caused by the man on this edge rotating his body in readiness to step forward on to left forward outside. Instead, he should follow the lady round so that the two bodies revolve as one, enabling him to step forward directly in front of his partner on to his 6th edge, left forward outside. As this edge is the first of a forward run for the man (left forward outside and right forward inside) at the same time as the lady is skating a backward run (right back outside – left back inside) this running movement has to be done with the man directly in front of the lady.

Before going on to step 8, I must say that step 4, for the lady and 4a and 4b, for the man can be delightful when done correctly but are so often performed very badly – the lady skating her 4-beat right forward outside edge with a static tracing knee and not rising as the man straightens his knee for his three turn and not sinking again with him as he sinks on to left back outside. This causes the heads to bob up and down. It is also all too common for the lady to have a very poorly turned out free leg with little, if any, toe point. See Plates 16 and 17 facing page 68.

Nor is the man blameless. We often see him cross over too deeply for his three turn causing his left shoulder to shoot forward. This makes him bend forward from the waist and results in an uncontrolled swinging three. In what appears to be a simple little movement like this there are many things which can upset the balance of the pair. These are the more usual ones at this stage and to go into the problem more deeply would only confuse the issue.

On step 8, left forward outside for the man and right back outside for the lady, the man directs his edge so that it will gradually bring him to the right of the lady for his cross-roll on to step 9. The right forward outside three turn, the lady doing a cross-roll on to left back outside. See Plate 18 facing page 68. While doing this edge the lady must take care not to rotate her body in readiness for step 10, right forward outside. If she does she will step forward to the left of the man completely blocking his path on step 10, left back outside. She should come forward directly in front of her partner and follow his edge round.

Steps 11a and 11b for the man are backward running steps and while he is doing this the lady is skating the left forward outside 2-beat edge which is the first edge of her closed mohawk turn. The lady should strike her 11th edge so that it runs parallel to the line of travel and slightly following the man's 11a and 11b. It is common for the lady to strike too far to her left on step 11 causing the bodies to be too far apart when she does the second edge of the mohawk – step 12, right back outside. When she makes the turn her left hip should come to the side of the man's right hip. Step 12 is a right back outside edge for both and as this is a 4-beat edge there is no necessity to pull it. If you place a true edge it will come round naturally. Care must be taken by both, at the completion of this edge, to see that the free foot is brought back to the instep of the tracing foot prior to striking forward on to the left forward inside edge – step 13. Often we see dancers falling on to this edge because they have only partially brought their free foot back to the tracing foot. The 14th and last step is a right forward inside edge. Many marks are lost in competition through dancers carelessly skating the last two edges, often skating either one or both on outsides.

Finally, a word about the lady's mohawk. This is a closed mohawk. The lady should strike on to her left forward outside edge, keeping her right hip back and as much weight as possible over the right foot to enable her to reach the ice comfortably with her right foot when placing it on to backward outside. When she brings her right foot up to the tracing foot, being a closed mohawk, she should bring it to the outside of the foot to enable her to place it on the ice close to the heel of the tracing foot and to move the tracing foot off the ice in front of her. Particular care must be taken not to bend forward.

The hold for this dance is the same as for the Waltz, although the bodies are not always facing one another.

I have described the lady's and man's steps together to enable either to refer to the particular part of the dance which is giving trouble and have a guide as to whether it is their fault or that of their partner.

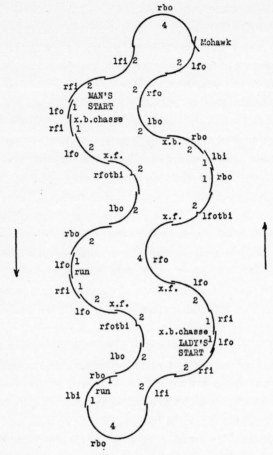

FIG 5 : *The Foxtrot*

The Foxtrot

Edges	Beats		Step No.	Edges	Beats	
	LADY'S STEPS			MAN'S STEPS		
LFO	1		1	LFO	1	
RFI	1	Cross Chassé	2	RFI	1	Cross Chassé
LFO	2		3	LFO	2	
RFO	4	Cross roll	4–4a	RFOTBI	2	Cross roll
			4b	LBO	2	
LFOTBI	2	Cross roll	5	RBO	2	
RBO	1		6	LFO	1	
LBI	1	Run	7	RFI	1	Run
RBO	2		8	LFO	2	Slight Tango Hold
LBO	2	Cross roll	9	RFOTBI	2	Cross roll
RFO	2	Slight change	10	LBO	2	Slight change of edge
LFO	2	Closed Mohawk to	11–11a	RBO	1	
			11b	LBI	1	Run
RBO	4		12	RBO	4	
LFI	2		13	LFI	2	
RFI	2		14	RFI	2	

CHAPTER NINE

The finer points necessary to pass the Bronze Medal Test

In dealing with the Bronze medal test I propose to point out the most usual mistakes dancers make while dancing their test, taking each dance separately in the order in which it is skated. Having explained the technical faults peculiar to each dance, I will then explain the test itself, giving a description of what is required of you in addition to doing the right steps, and the manner of procedure.

The British Fourteen-step

Although in Chapter 6 I have already dealt with double-tracking, this fault is of such importance that I feel I should impress it on your minds by going into the subject in greater detail here, since it is the mistake most common to the Fourteen-step. A dancer is double-tracking when he is travelling with two feet on the ice, both feet travelling in the same direction. There are many who ruin their dancing through not having a true knowledge of what double-tracking really is. You will see them trying to pick the tracing foot off the ice immediately the free foot comes up to the tracing foot, not allowing time for the push to take place. (To many this may seem obvious but let me assure you I often come across skaters who endeavour to do this, maybe because they have been told they must not double-track and, not having sufficient knowledge of what double-tracking really is, they try to pick one foot up as the other one goes down.) This makes the dancer snatch the foot off the ice in a most ungainly manner, losing all sense of rhythm and smoothness. To have two feet on the ice during the push is NOT double-tracking. You cannot push nothing along. This is what you are trying to do when you pick the tracing foot off the ice immediately the free foot arrives by its side for the push. When the push takes place, the body is pushed forward and in order for it to slide along the ice it must have something to slide on, which is the tracing foot. This is not double-tracking.

When the pushing foot turns out, it anchors on the ice to allow it to push against the ice, the body and tracing foot thereby being propelled forward or backward, as the case may be. Therefore the two feet are not travelling in the same direction. In the same way, you are not double-tracking when you have two feet on the ice while skating a mohawk. To perform a mohawk correctly the tracings should overlap, one foot travelling forward and the other travelling backward, the weight gradually transferring from one foot to the other without any kicking up of the free foot which would make an ugly, jerky movement when, if done correctly, it is as smooth as silk.

In this dance, time seems to defeat a number of people as the tempo is rather fast. They let the music run away with them and imagine they must rush in order to fit their steps in to the time of the music. One place where this frequently happens is on the seventh edge; right back outside for the lady, left forward outside for the man. There is plenty of time here as it is a two-beat edge. It may be caused by the man being a little shaky on his mohawk, which follows this edge, and thereby rushing to get it over, and the lady being over anxious to get from backward to forward. Their eagerness may prove their undoing, causing them to arrive too soon. A similar thing happens on the lady's twelfth edge; left forward outside first edge of the mohawk. When this happens it is usually a pointer to the lady's inability to do a good mohawk.

There is a great tendency in this dance for the lady to bend forward badly from the waist when doing the backward chassés. Doing so not only makes it difficult for her to

cross the left foot over the right correctly but will lose her
marks in the test through having bad carriage. There is also
a very strong tendency for her to bend forward from the waist
when moving from backward to forward on to her eighth
edge, left forward outside.

It is essential that the lady crosses her right foot behind
when doing her ninth edge, but when bending forward it is
extremely difficult to do. The man must take care to bring his
feet neatly together on his forward chassés and not to
double-track.

The Waltz

Bad time is most prominent in this dance. Although a
great number of dancers pay particular attention to placing
their skates down on the first beat of the bar when striking
forward, they are very inclined to lose sight of the fact that
they must turn the three on the right beat, which is the
third beat in the bar, and also place their skates down on
the first beat of the bar on the other edges if they wish to be
in time throughout the dance. It is very common to see
dancers turning the three on the second beat of the bar and
dropping on to the back edge too soon. You cannot honestly
say you are dancing if you are not dancing in time with
the music, therefore you will understand when I say that
time is a big factor in a dance test.

The less experienced dancer very often tries to strike forward as the partner turns the three – *Remember there is
another beat after that,* so be patient and wait until your
partner places down the following outside back edge and
strike on to your forward edge at the same time.

The Waltz being so simple in actual steps, it is necessary
to put the maximum amount of rhythm and movement into
the dance, plenty of rise and fall of the knee, combined with
strong, smooth and flowing edges. Try to keep in mind that
the Waltz done badly is a most uninteresting dance to watch

but done well it is difficult to find a dance to equal its flowing, graceful movement. Through its sheer simplicity it is more difficult to attain a really high standard in this dance than in any other.

When double-tracking occurs in this dance it is usually after the three turn.

One last word about the Waltz; treat it with respect, remember it is not only a Bronze dance. As you progress you have to skate it to a higher standard in the Inter-Silver, in the reverse direction of the rink and finally to a very high standard indeed in the Intermediate Gold Dance test.

The Foxtrot

The first stumbling block in this dance occurs in the opening chassé. In omitting to cross the right foot neatly behind the left then bringing the left foot to the side of the right before striking the next edge, left forward outside, this is often done untidily mainly due to the dancer bending forward. The lady seems to find more difficulty on her fourth and fifth steps, both of these being crossed in front, the fifth being more generally missed than the fourth. There is also a very great tendency for the lady to toe push whilst doing these steps, losing marks by so doing. Care must be taken to see that after the man's three turn, step No. 4a, until step No. 8, left forward outside, both partners remain directly in front of one another. So often we see them moving from side to side particularly when the lady does her three turn, step No. 5, and again when both are doing the running steps, Nos. 6 and 7. This is most important because it can lead to a failed test. As it is necessary for the partners to be hip to hip from the lady's twelfth step onwards, the lady must take care to strike her eleventh edge, left forward outside, in the same line as her partner's eleventh, right back outside, by skating a clean mohawk. Otherwise she will pull away from her partner, making it impossible for them to become hip to hip.

Care should be taken to avoid stepping wide on steps 13 and 14 and to make sure they are true inside edges.

You may wonder why I have taken the trouble to explain certain points in each dance during my review of the third class test, when I have already given a comprehensive description of each dance. The reason is they are points of which I want you to become really conscious. They have a nasty habit of going wrong when you are doing your test, even though you may normally do them quite correctly.

You must always bear in mind that nerves play a very big part in tests, often causing you to do things that you would never dream of doing under normal conditions. That is why it is always advisable to allow for a considerable drop in your standard when thinking of it in relation to a test.

When going in for your test, enter with complete confidence; this is such a help. If you find this difficult to do then think it over, and if there is any reason why you should lack confidence, carry on and do some more practice until you have rectified the trouble. There are few things more disappointing than to fail a test you have worked so hard to pass. If on the other hand you find there is no reason for your lack of confidence, go in with the feeling that you will do your best and try not to worry about it.

Having been thoroughly into the technical side of the dances, please do not think that it is only necessary to have good time and technical accuracy in order to pass your test. This is not the case. It is necessary to have personality and movement in your dancing, expressing the character of the dance you are performing. It is well to keep in mind when doing your test that the judges watch for inaccuracy of steps but are actually judging you from a dancing point of view and will not necessarily fail you for doing a wrong step. When the dancer warrants it, they will quite often explain the fault and allow them to do the dance again.

Plate 12 Correct position of free foot when about to turn a three. The man's big toe joint of the free foot in the hollow of the tracing foot. (Chapter 3, page 29)

Plate 13 Alignment of shoulders. Shoulders are not parallel in this photograph. It is particularly important when waltzing for the shoulders to remain parallel. (Chapter 3, page 32)

Plate 14 Correct pushing. Push with the outside edge when running backward, and forward. (Chapters 4 and 11, pages 34 and 70)

Plate 15 European Waltz. Hip protruding into the circle. (Chapter 7, page 50)

There are two judges for the Bronze dance test, who mark up to a maximum of six marks for each dance. The judges will, in the main, be looking for the following points :

(a) Time (including movements in unison to the time of the music), rise and fall of the tracing knee and rhythm.

(b) Style (which includes correct carriage and good form), with élan.

(c) Accuracy in steps, curves, edges turns and neatness of footwork.

It is stated in the Bye-Laws relating to Dancing on Ice, 'in order to pass the Bronze test a candidate must obtain from each judge a minimum of 2.8 for each dance and a minimum total of 10 marks for the three dances'.

In my experience I find few beginners read these Bye-Laws in their N.S.A. handbook and therefore know nothing about the method of judging. There are some, however, who do read them and it is not uncommon for them to think that if they receive 2.8 for each dance, then that is good enough. They have just not given any thought to the last part of the sentence which states : 'and a minimum of 10 marks'. This, of course, means that in order to pass you have to dance to 3.3 (to the nearest decimal point) on aggregate. Therefore, should you drop as low as 2.8 in one dance you make it necessary to dance one of the remaining dances to 3.8 or alternatively each of the two dances to 3.5 i.e.

Fourteen-step	2.8
Waltz	3.55
Foxtrot	3.55
	——
	9.90 to the nearest decimal point.
	——

It is not unusual to see a candidate skate a test with one weak dance and the other two just about up to standard. They are greatly disappointed when they fail. Do remember, however, that if you dance one dance to the minimum you are making it necessary to dance the other two to Inter-Silver standard, the pass mark for the higher test being 3.5. I often feel sorry for the judges when judging such a test because after the candidate has failed we often hear the remark, 'Look at "so and so". She passed and I am a better dancer than she is.'

I hope these few remarks will give you a better understanding of what is required of you to pass a test.

The test as it stands now is: Fourteen-step, Waltz and Foxtrot.

The candidate will be required to dance one dance on his or her own, this dance being chosen by the judges.

CHAPTER TEN

Reverse Waltz

Tempo 45 3/4

This is the first of the Intermediate Silver dances. The test consists of this dance, the International Fourteen-step, the Rocker foxtrot and a Variation dance.

Having described the Waltz in some detail in the Bronze dance test it will not be necessary for me to repeat the basic principles, the dance being exactly the same in pattern, edges and movement. The difference here is that it is danced the opposite way round the rink. It is, however, very necessary to draw your attention to the fact that the pass mark in this dance is higher, so a higher standard of performance is required in this test. This should follow quite naturally if you are practising on the right lines.

The first three tests are graded to allow the pupil through a small improvement to steadily progress through their tests, the pass mark rising very gradually. Preliminary Bronze: minimum mark 2.5, pass mark 3.0, Bronze: minimum mark 2.8, pass mark 3.3, Intermediate Silver : minimum mark 3.0, pass mark 3.5. It will be seen that half a mark covers the three tests. I am mentioning this now because rapid progress is made by many up to Inter-Silver and if, as is often the case, the pupil has gone in for the Inter-Silver test and passed it but only just, they have a long and tedious task ahead of them before they can pass their Silver – minimum mark jumping from 3.0 to 3.5 and the pass mark from 3.5 to 4.0. You will see that the improvement required from Inter-Silver to Silver is a half mark, which is the equivalent of the improvement required for the whole of the three previous tests.

In view of the above, the best way to progress through all

the dance tests happily and without unhappy failures, is to practice until you are at least 25 per cent better than the required standard before attempting to pass the test. This will allow for nerves, allow you to go in in a better frame of mind and will reduce the period of time between tests.

Few pupils find the reverse Waltz, to begin with, as easy as the ordinary Waltz, although it is basically the same. There are several reasons for this. Few rinks these days have a period of reverse skating. The Reverse Waltz requires the pupil to skate successive three turns round the end of the rink on the right foot, which should not create any real difficulty but it does, mainly because, when learning the Preliminary Waltz, you are required to turn a left three only. In the Bronze Waltz in the average rink you skate one right three on either side of the rink only, followed by successive left threes round the ends of the rink all of which adds up to more practice on left threes than right threes. This of course is where the figure skater scores against the non figure skater.

How do I attain the Higher Standard Required?

Firstly, improve the co-ordination of movement by pushing smoothly and allowing the tracing knee to bend slowly in the same timing as the push. Secondly, by slowly straightening the tracing knee and drawing the free leg up to the tracing leg so that they are both moving in the same timing with the feet arriving together just in time for the next stroke, without any rush. Thirdly, by improving the turn-out and toe point of the free leg. Fourthly, by neater foot-work, bringing your feet together for the turns, placing your feet neatly together when changing from one foot to the other and lastly, by paying greater attention to your deportment, making sure you keep your head up and not bending forwards or backwards.

Plate 16 TOP LEFT: Bad free leg by the lady on the fourth edge of the Foxtrot. (Chapter 8, page 56) *Plate* 17 TOP RIGHT: Correct free leg on the fourth edge of the Foxtrot. (Chapter 8, page 56) *Plate* 18 LEFT: Body position striking step 9 in the Foxtrot. (Chapter 8, page 56)

Plate 19 Completion of swing through in the International
Fourteen-step. (Chapter 11, page 71)

CHAPTER ELEVEN

The International Fourteen-Step

Music and Tempo :
March 2/4 or 6/8 at 56 bars per minute
March 4/4 at 28 bars per minute

This, as its name implies, is an international dance – which means it is accepted by the International Skating Union, the recognised world governing body of ice skating. Should you be visiting another country, the Fourteen-step you will see skated will be the dance I am about to describe, and as this is a set-pattern dance it would be wrong to go on and dance the British version which is a round dance, as it would interfere with the other dancers.

When we say 'set-pattern dance' this means it is danced in the pattern as laid down by the governing body, each sequence following exactly the same pattern as the first. The pattern for this dance is clearly shown in Figs. 6 and 7 at the end of this chapter.

The character of this dance is similar in every way to the British Fourteen-step, with this difference; the first two steps in the British version form a chassé, whilst the first two in the International form a run, and the fourth edge, being a four-beat edge, forms a deep lobe or curve, commencing towards the centre of the rink and gradually bringing the dancers back to the barrier to commence the fifth edge the same distance away from the barrier as in the first step. Having described the similarities of the two Fourteen-steps I will now describe in detail the slight difference in steps and manner of performance.

As previously stated, the dancers are allowed up to seven steps of their own choice to bring them in to the dance hold and to position them in the right part of the rink for commencing the dance. Particular care must be taken when commencing the dance that the man is directly in front of the lady, neither to her right or left, in the Waltz hold. This is most important because should either partner move slightly to the side they will be marked down. It is particularly stressed that while dancing the first seven edges the dancers should be directly in front of one another.

Having arrived in the correct dancing position the lady strikes her first edge – right back outside and the man, left forward outside – towards the barrier, forming the first part of the run which is completed by step number 2 – left back inside for the lady and right forward inside for the man. Care must be taken by the man when he is striking on to right forward inside not to toe-push – a very common fault which is avoided by turning the left toe in for the push with the weight on the front of the skate and pushing with the outside edge. See Plate No. 14 opposite page 65. He must also be sure the right foot passes the left or it will not be a running movement. The lady also has a difficult striking action when striking on to her second edge – left back inside – she often just slips the right foot forward off the ice with the toe stuck up in the air in a most ungainly and sloppy manner with no push whatsoever. In order to make the running push the lady must first of all make sure she maintains a strong right outside edge to enable her to turn the right foot out and give an outside push on to her second edge – left back inside. Care must once more be exercised to see that the left foot passes the right or it will not be a run. It is very common for the lady to do more of a slip step than a run.

So much for the first two edges which, having started moving towards the barrier, will gradually curve away from it. The third edge, right back outside for the lady and left forward outside for the man, is struck in the same line as the previous edge and, curving to the left, will bring the dancers towards the centre of the rink and complete the first lobe of the dance.

The word 'lobe' is commonly used in ice skating but I have purposely not referred to it before, there being sufficient to think about in the early stages. However, we are now at the intermediate stage of ice dancing and for the benefit of the younger dancers I must explain that the term lobe is used to describe a part of a circle or, as described in my dictionary, 'any rounded and projecting part'. Reference to Figs 6 and 7 will make it clear that there are three lobes on each side of the rink in the Fourteen-step, one inner lobe and two outer lobes. While talking about lobes I must mention that the two outer lobes should be so placed that if we drew a straight line from the apex of one lobe to the apex of the other, the line drawn would be parallel to the barrier.

We now move to step 4 – left back outside edge for the lady and right forward outside edge for the man. These edges should be struck in the same line of travel as the previous edge, the new skating foot being placed on the ice close to the pushing foot. This edge will progress towards the centre of the rink and at its apex, or centre of the curve, will gradually curve back towards the barrier. During the skating of these edges, the lady's free leg swings, in a controlled manner, from in front to behind the tracing leg, returning to the side of the skating foot for the next stroke. Likewise, the man's left leg will swing from behind, past the skating leg, and back to the tracing foot for the next stroke. Care must be taken here that the lady's and the man's free legs move exactly together and are well turned out with the toe pointed. See Plate 19 between pages 68–69.

Steps 5, 6 and 7 are a repetition of steps 1, 2 and 3 and are skated in exactly the same way. The lady must be careful on her seventh edge not to over-rotate her body in readiness for striking forward on to her eighth edge, left forward outside. Should she do so she will tend to hook her edge into the centre and away from her partner causing the shoulders to come out of parallel with one another so making it impossible for the two bodies to revolve smoothly together. It also makes it difficult for her to strike forward on to the outside edge, hence the reason why we often see the lady strike an inside edge. The man on his seventh edge must take care to follow exactly in line with the lady's edge, and be most careful not to strike out of the cricle when striking his eighth edge, right forward inside, – the first edge of his mohawk. Should he do so, he will pull away from his partner, making both bodies bend forward from the waist and making it virtually impossible for him to skate his mohawk correctly.

The rest of the International Fourteen-step is the same as the British Fourteen-step, with this difference: the forward steps for the lady and the backward steps for the man must be skated round the end of the rink when skating the International as this is a set-pattern dance, whereas the British, being optional pattern, progresses round the circle with the steps coming in a slightly different place each time. I must mention, however, that in this test the judges will expect more attention to be paid to the relative positions of the two bodies. While skating steps 8, 9, 10, 11, 12 and 13, the lady should be facing out of the circle and the man into the circle, the hips and shoulders being, so far as is possible, flat, or parallel to the tracing. To make it possible for the dancers to maintain the body positions required, it will be necessary for the lady to ensure that she keeps her right hip back when she strikes forward on to her eighth edge, left forward outside which will enable her to maintain this position up to and including her mohawk. Incidentally, by so doing, it will make it much easier for her to do her Mohawk. The man, when skating the left back inside edge of his open mohawk, step 9, must be particularly careful to check back his right hip to enable him to skate these backward edges in the required position.

Rise and fall is very necessary in every dance but in a fast moving dance like the Fourteen-step, with the exception of the fourth edge – a four-beat edge – it is better to skate it with a soft knee and ankle action and allow the knee bend to be dictated by the feel of the music. This, if you can acquire it, will give a more undulating movement as if gliding over waves.

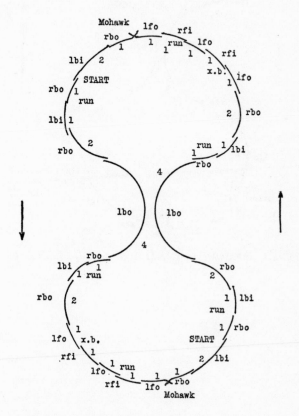

FIG 6 : *The Fourteen-step (International) Lady's steps*

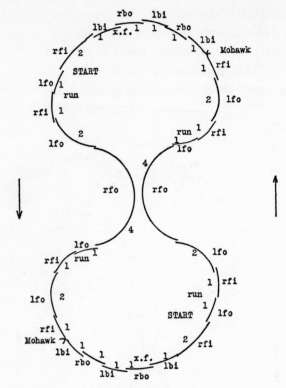

FIG 7 : *The Fourteen-step (International) Man's steps*

The Fourteen-Step (*International*)

	LADY'S STEPS			MAN'S STEPS		
Edges	*Beats*		*Step No.*	*Edges*	*Beats*	
RBO	1		1	LFO	1	
LBI	1	Run	2	RFI	1	Run
RBO	2		3	LFO	2	
LBO	4	Free leg swing	4	RFO	4	Free leg swing
RBO	1		5	LFO	1	
LBI	1	Run	6	RFI	1	Run
RBO	2		7	LFO	2	
LFO	1		8	RFI	1	Open
						Mohawk to
RFI	1	Cross behind	9	LBI	1	
LFO	1		10	RBO	1	
RFI	1	Run	11	LBI	1	Run
LFO	1	Open	12	RBO	1	
		Mohawk to				
RBO	1		13	LBI	1	Cross-in-front
LBI	2		14	RFI	2	

CHAPTER TWELVE

The Rocker Foxtrot

Music and Tempo : Foxtrot 4/4 at 26 bars per minute

International Dance

The Rocker Foxtrot is the *bête noire* of the lady who attempts it before she has complete mastery of the rudiments of skating. Although it is not expected of her to do a perfectly clean rocker (that is to say without having a double line) it *is* expected that she should do it without a terrific skid! To do a good rocker does not mean that you must be up to Gold standard for, though it is a Gold figure, in the dance it is done more like a free skating rocker. Even so, if we are to produce a good result, complete control and a strong edge is necessary. A little explanation of the rocker as required in the dance, might be advisable before going any further with the description of the dance.

The rotation is the same as for the figure rocker, but it must in no way give the appearance of a figure turn. This would be altogether too cramped for dancing, there being only one beat allowed up to the cusp of the turn. The cusp of the turn is the actual mark made on the ice as the skate turns from forward outside to backward outside (See Fig. 8).

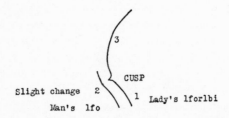

FIG 8 : *The Rocker Foxtrot – the fifth edge showing the Lady's rocker and the Man's 2 beat L.F.O. edge*

Plate 20 The man dropping right shoulder of sixth edge of the Rocker Foxtrot. (Chapter 12, page 79)

Plate 21 Correct striking of sixth edge in the Rocker Fox-trot. (Chapter 12, page 79)

Plate 22 TOP LEFT: The Tango – wrong hold. The lady's arm is too straight, resulting in the man having to reach over. (Chapter 16, page 94) *Plate* 23 TOP RIGHT: The Tango – correct hold. (Chapter 16, page 94) *Plate* 24 RIGHT: The Tango. Free leg between partner. (Chapter 16, page 95)

The rocker turn requires a very strong edge indeed to enable you to maintain the outside edge both on the forward and backward part of the figure. A very strong rotation of the hips is also required for a rocker, to enable you to turn the tracing foot sufficiently to come out of the turn on the same edge as you go into it. The rotation is made by rotating the hips on top of the tracing leg so that the right hip will come forward. This rotation has to be made very quickly to enable the lady to turn on the second beat, and whilst making this rotation the free foot should be brought up to and slightly past the tracing foot so that it is just in front of the tracing foot as the rocker is turned. In order not to impede the rotation of the hips, care must be taken that the free foot passes the tracing foot without any turn out.

As all this takes place in the space of one beat of music there is no obvious lack of turn out, particularly as the free foot takes up a turned out position immediately the rocker is turned. As the turn of the left foot is in an anti-clockwise direction, by not having any turn out of the free foot as the rocker is turned, and by allowing it to follow the tracing foot round as it turns – providing you do not let it go too far – it will be turned out on completion of the turn. This may be a little difficult for you to understand but I have no doubt, after a little experimenting, you will see the point. After the rocker has been turned, the free leg is stretched out behind you, well turned out and toe pointed. It is then brought forward past the tracing and in front of the tracing foot to match the man's free leg while he is skating right forward outside, both bringing the feet together at the end of the stroke.

I have explained the rocker movement for the lady first, before explaining the dance, because through years of experience I have always found this to be the best approach to learning the dance.

When this dance was invented by E. L. Keats and E.

Van der Weyden, it was well thought-out. In those days there was no such thing as a set pattern dance. If started in the right place it fits the rink perfectly, taking the length of the rink for the sequence of steps, so that the rocker and mohawks come in the same place each time. On the other hand, should you start the dance in the wrong place it becomes almost impossible to do without deviating from the correct shape, the first five edges being all on the same curve. Therefore unless you start round the end of the rink they will bring you right across the centre, while to deviate from the course of the dance would necessitate doing wrong edges. This now being a set pattern dance, a little study of the pattern as laid down, will more than pay for the time expended on it. The best place to start is so that your first steps – left forward outside chassé – commence in the centre at the end of the rink.

It will be seen from Fig. 9 page 81, that the Rocker Foxtrot starts with a cross behind chassé immediately followed by a run, the first four edges being one-beat edges and the fifth, two beats for the man and one beat (leading up to the rocker) for the lady, with three beats following the turn. Up to the fifth edge the lady does exactly the same edges as the man. The run following immediately on the last edge of the chassé often causes a little confusion when this dance is first attempted; having to do four edges in four beats has the psychological effect of making you hurry the steps, but I assure you there is plenty of time to do the edges without hurrying them. In the case of the lady, of course, she is thinking only of the rocker which is following, to the exclusion of everything else, often even to the exclusion of the preparation for the rocker. A very good plan is to practise the chassé and run without the rocker – not forgetting to cross behind on the second edge, right forward inside and to bring the left foot to the side of the right for the next edge – until you become accustomed to doing it in the right time. The lady would be well advised to practise the rocker on her own so that she does not become used to relying on the man to hold her up, which is a bad habit to get into and even worse to correct. When practising the chassé and run, let the edge come well round but do not strike into the circle, the lady being particularly careful not to try and force ahead of her partner.

Presuming you are now reasonably sure of the first four edges, proceed with the rocker. The left edge into the rocker should be curved as much as the time allowed for the edge will permit; however, the left forward outside edge should be progressing slightly towards the centre of the rink when the rocker is turned and the edge out of the rocker MUST be very strong, curving well back to the barrier. The man must take care with his two-beat fifth edge to follow the line of the lady's left forward outside rocker, because the lady turns her rocker after one beat and the man is skating a two-beat left forward outside edge, he will have to straighten the curve during the second beat to follow the line of the lady's rocker. The rise and fall of the man's tracing knee must be in unison with the lady while doing the rocker.

On the man's sixth edge, right forward outside, care should be taken not to drop the right shoulder which gives a very ugly appearance and often causes the free leg to swing out wide with the knee turned in and the heel stuck up in the air. The man should be careful to strike his sixth edge straight on in the same line as the previous edge, following the same curve as the lady makes with the back outside edge of her rocker. See Plates 20 and 21 between pages 76–77. The man's seventh edge, left forward outside three back inside, should be struck with the feet together not, as is so often the case, with the left foot crossed in front of the right; if it is, it causes a definite pulling away from the lady, her corresponding edge, right back outside, being placed by the side.

While the man is skating his eighth and ninth edges, right

back outside and left forward outside (both edges being of two beats duration), the lady is doing her seventh edge, left forward outside edge of four beats duration. As the man is doing a backward edge followed by a forward edge while the lady holds her long left forward outside edge, it is advisable for her to hold her free leg back for three beats to enable the two free legs to move up to the tracing foot together in readiness for the next edge. While the man is skating these two edges he will rise and fall on each edge, so care must be taken by the lady to see that she rises and falls with the man – which means she will rise and fall twice on her four-beat edge.

For the rest of the dance the edges are the same for both, particular care being taken to see your skate is running exactly parallel with your partner's skate. The right forward outside edge must be crossed in front and struck towards the centre. The following edge, left forward inside, must also be crossed in front bringing you slightly round on your course back to the barrier. On these two edges there is a definite tendency to lift up the feet as though you are stepping over something; it is a very ugly movement and takes away from the rhythm of the dance tremendously.

The right forward outside edge preceding the left forward outside edge of the mohawk, is struck towards the barrier. It is very common to see this outside edge change and become an inside edge; this is usually caused by striking the left forward outside edge of the mohawk too straight down the rink instead of in the same line as the previous edge, which should be slightly towards the barrier. When this happens it usually causes a nasty side lurch onto the left forward outside edge of the mohawk. Thus it is not uncommon to see this become an inside edge, making a choctaw instead of a mohawk. The right backward edge of the mohawk must be a definite outside edge, coming sufficiently round to allow the left backward inside edge (which is crossed

in front) and the right forward inside edge, to bring you up
to the centre, ready to repeat the dance.

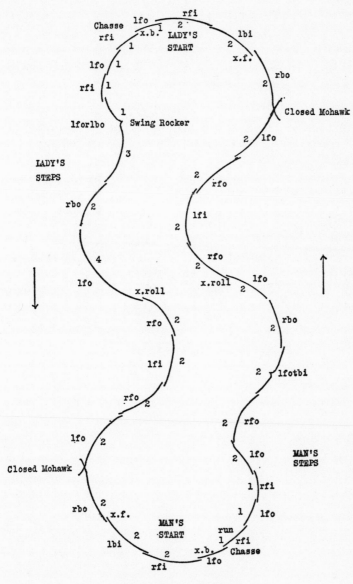

FIG 9: *Rocker Foxtrot*

The Rocker Foxtrot

	LADY'S STEPS		Step No.	MAN'S STEPS		
Edges	*Beats*			*Edges*	*Beats*	
LFO	1		1	LFO	1	
RFI	1	Cross behind chassé	2	RFI	1	Cross behind chassé
LFO	1		3	LFO	1	
RFI	1	Run	4	RFI	1	Run
LFO	1	Swing Rocker to	5–5a	LFO	2	
LBO	3		5–5b	RFO	2	
RBO	2		6	LFOTBI	2	Feet together for push
LFO	4		7–7a	RBO	2	
			7b	LFO	2	
RFO	2	Cross roll	8	RFO	2	Cross roll
LFI	2	Run	9	LFI	2	Run
RFO	2		10	RFO	2	
LFO	2	Closed Mohawk to	11	LFO	2	Closed Mohawk to
RBO	2		12	RBO	2	
LBI	2	Cross-in-front	13	LBI	2	Cross-in-front
RFI	2		14	RFI	2	

CHAPTER THIRTEEN

Variation Dance

In my opinion this would be better called a 'variation of a dance' because this is, in fact, what it is. You are required to make up a variation of your own choice and incorporate it into the Bronze Foxtrot or any one of the dances in the Silver Test.

The variation must be of a minimum of 6 bars and a maximum of 20 bars. This variation may commence on any step of the chosen dance, with the proviso that you are able, at the end of the variation, to go back into the chosen dance where you left off and dance the remainder of the dance. You must then repeat the dance and variation – the variation starting and finishing on the same step as in the first sequence.

Effect timing and rhythm are more important in the variation than difficulty.

Remember a dance is not necessarily a good dance because it is difficult. A dance is very good when it is both pleasing to watch and enjoyable to dance.

The variation may be made up of any dance steps, turns, changes of edge etc., and may be further enhanced, should the step warrant it, by changes of hold. It must be understood, however, that you have to come back into the hold of the chosen dance when you move back from the variation into the original dance.

Note. A simple, flowing, free moving variation presented well, is more likely to catch the eye of the judges than a difficult, cramped variation which does not blend in freely with the dance chosen.

CHAPTER FOURTEEN

The Intermediate Silver Dance Test

Having made application to the National Skating Association of Great Britain to become a candidate for the Intermediate Silver Dance test you will, in due course, receive a card from the N.S.A. rink representative stating that your test will take place, normally, at the rink of your choice at a given time. If you are unable to comply with the instructions on the card you should notify your rink representative as soon as possible and if you have reasonable grounds for not taking your test at the time or place stated, you will be tested on some future occasion. A test does sometimes have to be postponed for a considerable time, either through illness or a slight accident of some kind, and fortunately the N.S.A., in their Bye-Laws, have made provision for this i.e. Should you have made application to be tested for your Inter-Silver Dance test in, say, February and for some unforseen reason you are unable to take the test before the end of the test year, 1st June (there being a closed season between 1st June and 1st September, when no tests will take place other than for foreign visitors or professionals) you will be allowed until 31st January of the following year to take it.

Up to and including the Inter-Silver dance test you will be judged by two judges, from there on by three. It may be gratifying for you to know that they too have satisfied the N.S.A. Ice Dance Committee that they are capable of judging to the higher standard before being put on the register of judges for the higher tests. For instance, a First Class judge may judge any test but a lesser qualified judge may only judge tests up to the standard he has been appointed, with this exception : in special cases where it is not possible to get two judges of the required standard it is

84

possible for the senior judge to co-opt a judge from the lower panel of judges (providing he is satisfied that such a judge is up to it) to complete the panel of judges.

Therefore, not only have you to skate your test to a higher standard than in the previous test but the judges also have to be of a higher standard, every precaution being taken to see you are tested fairly.

In order to pass the test you have to satisfy BOTH judges that you are up to the required standard and, as I have previously stated, should you dance one dance to the minimum standard allowed, you will be required to dance the rest of the dances to a higher standard to make up the aggregate which is 14 marks for the four dances, or 3.5 for each dance. *For your own sake as well as that of the judges, do see you are at least capable of dancing each dance to the required standard before applying for a test.* Judges do not like failing you any more than you like failing.

In order to pass the test you have to dance to a slightly higher standard than for the Bronze test. You might ask 'why make such an obvious statement?' I will tell you why. Many aspirants to test honours are under the misapprehension of thinking that when they are able to dance, easily and comfortably, the new dances they have learned for the new test they are ready to go in for their next test – believing the higher test just consists of more difficult dances. This is not the case, of course, as the dances in the higher tests are not necessarily more difficult. In fact, you will sometimes come across a dance in the higher tests which is quite simple in actual steps but needs a considerably higher standard of dancing to show it off. For instance, the International Waltz is danced in our Bronze Medal Test and also in the Gold. You will see therefore it is not your ability to dance more intricate steps which will get you the pass mark of the test, but your ability to dance and move with ever increasing relaxation, rhythm and grace, bearing in mind that as you progress through the higher tests, the dances you were previously tested on should correspondingly improve in standard.

COMMON FAULTS IN THIS TEST

WALTZ. Bad timing, untidy footwork and poor carriage of the free leg and, in particular, stiffness and general lack of movement. These faults are very prevalent in the Waltz but to a slightly lesser degree they apply to the following dances as well.

FOURTEEN-STEP (INTERNATIONAL). Not running directly in front of your partner. Making more of a slip step or half chassé of the running movement instead of a clear cut run. Bad interpretation of the set pattern of the dance. Inferior mohawks.

ROCKER FOXTROT. Where applicable, as in the previous two dances with the following additions : Failing to bring the feet together after the crossed behind chassé at the beginning of the dance. Weak rocker by the lady. The man failing to follow the line of travel of the lady's rocker, causing bad alignment of the bodies and generally impairing the movement and style of the dancers. This dance should be danced with plenty of freedom and movement, the lack of this is often very apparent. Poor mohawks.

VARIATION. On the whole, I very rarely have to criticise the general conception of the variation danced in a test and in fact I have seen some very pleasing variations indeed. Where criticism is necessary it is usually the general standard of the dancing of the variation which is at fault, though there are occasions when the variation is obviously too difficult for the dancer. Do remember that the pleasing effect of a variation is more important than the difficulty.

* * *

When deciding which dance to use for the variation choose the rhythm you like the most or the dance which gives you the most pleasure to dance. This way you will put it over much better. Also, remember a simple rhythm like the Foxtrot is easier to put over than the more difficult rhythm of the Tango.

CHAPTER FIFTEEN

The American Waltz

Music and Tempo : 3/4 at 66 bars per minute

This is an International dance and it is stated to be a preferred pattern dance. However, so far as the preferred pattern
is concerned, it would be as well to forget it for the only
preference one is allowed are the number of lobes we are
to skate along the sides of the rink. It is clearly stated that
in rinks of less than 57 metres (187 feet) only one lobe will
be skated to the midline of the rink making three lobes in
all along the side of the rink, and in rinks of 57 metres and
over, two lobes to the midline of the rink will be required,
making five lobes in all along the side of the rink. This
really means that the only variation of pattern allowed is
governed by the size of the rink – in other words, more or
less lobes according to the size of the ice surface. The actual
formation, however, of these lobes is very set indeed, therefore, in my opinion the words 'Preferred Pattern' are somewhat misleading. Woe betide anyone who decides to skate
continuous threes around the ends of the rink as in the
International Waltz.

In my view the American Waltz could be said to be a
development of the International Waltz. By this I do not
mean to infer that it is in any way superior to the International Waltz but that in basic principles they are very
similar, each dance being skated by three edges in a clockwise direction followed by three edges skated in an anti-
clockwise direction. The lady in both cases skating a forward
outside three followed by two backward outside edges and
the man skating two forward outside edges followed by a
forward outside three-turn. This is where the similarity ends.

The American Waltz, being based on six beat edges, calls for a different usage of the free legs and thereby a different technique in the performance of the dance.

As in all dances, the steps leading into the dance are left to the choice of the dancers. With the American Waltz, however, I always think it better to start with the orthodox six-beat open edges with the leg swing, followed by the lady's three turn, bringing the couple into the Waltz hold. Doing the six-beat edges with the swing of the legs immediately gives you the feel of the rhythm.

One of the fundamental principles of the American Waltz is that the free leg should be *about* to pass the tracing leg on the count of four but on no account should the free foot *pass* the tracing foot on this count nor should there by any hesitation of the swing of the free leg. The timing of the swing of the leg should be such as will cause it to be just about to pass on the count of four with a smooth flowing action. Likewise, when turning the three the free foot should not pass the tracing foot before the turn but, again, should be about to pass so that the feet will be close together when the turn is made (though not touching) so that the general effect once more is a smooth swing of the free leg. Great care should be applied while making the three turn with the swing of the free leg, in fact it is often one of the weakest or most untidy parts of the dance. I shall therefore proceed to explain the movement in detail :

The reason so much care is required is because when you turn the three the free foot is approximately slightly to the back of the tracing foot. It will be seen that if it remains where it is whilst the three is being turned it will automatically be carried about the width of your shoulders along the line of travel. Should you swing the leg through while you are turning, the turning of the three will add to the swing and cause you to have an unbalanced swing of the leg, giving the effect of kicking up at the back after the turn.

To avoid this the clever dancer will slightly restrict the movement of the free leg while turning, without it being perceptible, and just stretch it behind him after the turn with no apparent break in the movement.

The swing of the free leg of both partners must be synchronised. If the bending and straightening of the tracing knee is synchronised to the swing of the free leg it will considerably assist the partners in keeping their movements together and will add to the flow of the dance. This synchronising is best done in the following way : striking on to the new edge with both knees straight, the knee bend will take place throughout the push on the first beat. The straightening of the knee should coincide with the moving or swing of the free leg so that the movement will be performed smoothly and without rush. At the completion of the edge the free foot is brought up to the tracing foot on the count of six in readiness for the next stroke.

In this dance, as in the International Waltz, it is essential that the shoulders and hips should remain parallel with one another throughout the dance, making sure at the same time that there is no side movement of the bodies. For example; the man's right shoulder should always be directly opposite the lady's left shoulder and likewise his left directly opposite her right, the two bodies revolving as if attached to one another, or as though revolving on a centre pin directly in the middle between the two bodies.

It is pretty obvious, but worthy of mention, that as the free legs play such a big part in this dance, they should always be well turned out with the toe pointed. Failure to maintain the turn-out completely ruins the dance.

Great care should also be taken with the deportment in this dance as there is a strong tendency, probably due to the swing of the free legs, for the partners to bend forward from the waist, giving a disastrous effect.

It will be seen from the above that whilst this dance can

be most attractive to watch, it can also be one of the ugliest. Considerable care must be maintained in its execution.

The tempo is 3/4 timing, or three beats to the bar, but as each edge in the American Waltz is skated to six beats, the music is played so as to give slightly more emphasis to the first beat of the first and third bars in each four bar phrase of music. This emphasis, however, is only *slightly* marked and it is necessary, therefore, to listen carefully before commencing the dance to make sure you move off on the strongly marked bar. Failure to move off on the strongly marked bar completely spoils the effect and to the musically minded jars considerably, looking as if you are skating on the off-beat although you are not really out of time but are out of rhythm or phrasing.

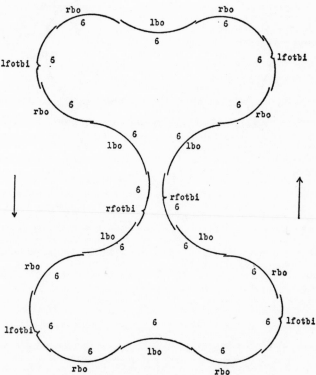

FIG 10 : *American Waltz – Lady's steps*

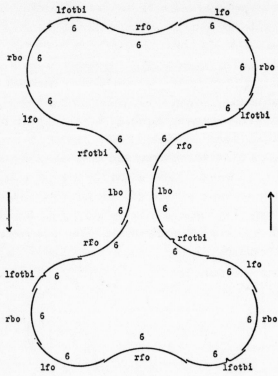

FIG 11 : *American Waltz – Man's steps*

CHAPTER SIXTEEN

The Tango

Music and Tempo : 4/4 at 27 bars per minute

This is an International Dance. Preferred pattern

Those of you who have a copy of my earlier book on ice dancing will observe that the tempo of this dance has since been changed from 22 bars per minute to 27. This came about when it was decided to change the linking edges between the chassés to four beat edges instead of two beat edges; however, basically the dance remains the same although the alteration from two beat to four beat edges does alter the carriage of the free legs on the four beat edges. This I will explain later.

The Tango, being a dance possibly stronger in character than any other, gives the real expert a chance to shine by expressing the strong rhythm and character of the dance in the movements, so showing his or her ability at its best. Although it is such a good dance for showing the ability of the good dancer it is equally good at showing the inability of the less fortunate. I say less fortunate because the really good dancer does more than just perform the steps well. He has personality in every movement, is the type of person you just cannot help looking at, even though he may be less accurate than other dancers. Whether it is a lady or gentleman who is gifted with this natural dancing ability, they are extremely lucky for, with good tuition to combine the technical with the natural, there are no heights they cannot attain. Unfortunately, this type of dancer rarely takes the fullest advantage of his or her good fortune by combining the technical with the natural. Consequently it is not uncommon for the person who has just medium dancing ability to beat them through correct guidance and hard work, although it may be more tedious for them and take them some time to attain the standard.

The Tango with its many crossed steps, both in front and behind, and its rotation (so that first your right hip and shoulder is touching your partner's right hip and shoulder, then the left hips and shoulders are touching, and so on four times) presents considerable difficulty to some, while others fall into it quite easily. In most cases this depends on the SKATING ability of the person trying to do the dance.

The hold for the Tango is the same throughout as for the Waltz. Although the hold must be firm it must not be stiff, in order to allow the body to rotate easily without any pull on your partner. It is also necessary to keep the shoulder and elbow joints flexible without allowing the arms to be unsteady and limp. Many people dancing the Tango try to do the impossible. I have previously stated that at certain parts of the dance the partners have alternately their right and then their left hips and shoulders together. Although they are not jammed tightly together it is not uncommon to see both partners trying to keep their right arm (for the lady) and left arm (for the man) straight out with their corresponding shoulders together. This, of course, is the impossible part and leads to shockingly distorted positions. In order to perform this movement correctly, when the right shoulders are together the man must allow his left elbow to bend, otherwise the lady's extended right hand cannot possibly reach the man's extended left hand. When the left hips and shoulders are together the lady will of course have to allow her right elbow to bend. Please see Plates 22 and 23 facing page 77.

The dance is usually started by the lady and the man taking first a left edge and then a right edge. The lady then turns a left outside three towards the off-side barrier, the man following her line of travel. This will bring her in front of her partner and is followed by a right backward outside edge which will bring the couple towards the centre of the rink ready for the first edges of the dance – left backward outside crossed behind, for the lady and right forward outside crossed in front for the man. The second step for the lady is right backward inside crossed in front chassé, the second step for the man being left forward inside crossed behind chassé. Edges one and two are each of one beat duration. This is the first time the dancers become shoulder to shoulder and hip to hip. I use the term 'shoulder to shoulder and hip to hip' to emphasise that there must not be any appreciable space between the bodies at this stage, but do not take me too literally : you should not be rigidly jammed together! In the official description of the dance it states 'side-by-side'. However, any appreciable gap will cause one or the other to bend sideways and will consequently lose marks.

A very common fault when performing the side-by-side movements in this dance is for the one who is going forward to progress too far forward, causing him to be too far to the back of his partner, making it impossible for the bodies to smoothly rotate and co-ordinate with one another on the subsequent four beat edge.

The feet are brought together by both for the third edge, left backward edge for the lady and right forward edge for the man. This is the first of the four beat edges. The lady must take particular care when moving on to her third edge because her pushing foot must come off the ice directly in front of her so that at the completion of the stroke her free leg will be between her and her partner, or on the outside of her partner's right leg as shown in the photograph. See Plate 24 facing page 77. During the skating of this four beat edge both bodies slowly rotate as the edge progresses towards the barrier. At the completion of the third beat the free legs are brought smartly through ready to be crossed behind by the lady and crossed in front by the man, for edge number four.

In recent years it has become quite fashionable to make a momentary pause with the free leg as it passes the tracing leg, before proceeding to its crossed position. This method of moving the free leg through has certain advantages, the main one being that it is easier for the partners to move their free legs together with a slight break in the movement half way. In my opinion the movement of the bodies and the free legs on the four beat edges can greatly enhance the character of the dance. Therefore, I prefer the following method: when the four beat edge is commenced on the first beat in the bar, delay the rotation of the body and movement of the free leg until fractionally before the count of four, to allow both body and free leg to move smartly through so that the free leg will arrive in front of the tracing foot just in time to be crossed in front on the count of one. When the four beat edge commences on the third beat in the bar, the movement of body and free leg will take place fractionally before the count of two. The same applies when moving backwards, with this difference: the free foot of the partner proceeding backwards will be crossed behind. At the completion of the crossed chassé the free foot is brought to the side of the tracing foot; here again, if the free foot is brought from the crossed position to the side of the tracing foot smartly, it once more adds character to the dance – one of the characteristics of the Tango being long drawn out movements followed by short, sharp staccato movements.

It will be seen, therefore, that a certain amount of licence is permitted to allow the individual to show his or her personality. When skating the crossed steps, care must be taken not to curve them too much or there will be little curve left for the four beat edge following, because the four beat edge must not come back across the short axis.

Proceed with steps 4, 5 and 6 in the same ways as for 1, 2

Plate 25 The Kilian – wrong position on step 14, showing the man unable to get his right foot through. (Chapter 17, page 106)

Plate 26 The Kilian – correct position on step 14. (Chapter 17 page 106)

Plate 27 Back outside upright spiral (Chapter 19, page 120)

and 3. The lady must be careful on her seventh edge, left backward outside (crossed behind) not to pull the edge round too sharply or she will find it difficult to come forward to the right-hand side of her partner with her eighth step, right forward outside, also causing the man to have difficulty in doing his seventh edge, right forward outside three backward inside, into the centre of the rink. The man must be careful not to swing his three or he will not be able to keep the line of progression towards the centre. The man's three is taken very shallow; in fact it is not really a true turn at all. It is more often seen turned on a flat or forced edge. During the performing of the three turn the man takes his free leg forward as, or slightly before, he makes the turn. He must control the free leg so as to be ready for his eighth edge, left backward outside (crossed behind) or he will most likely be late placing down.

The lady places her eighth edge down as the man does left backward outside (crossed behind). Care should be taken here as we often see the lady try to come forward as the man does his three, putting her out of time with the music. The lady should come forward to the right of the man and proceed with steps 9, 10, 11, 12, 13 and 14, in the same way as for the previous edges, with the exception that the lady's three turn (step 14) is slightly rounder than was the man's three turn on step 7. While the lady is skating her three the man must be careful, while skating his corresponding edge, left backward outside, not to hook it round or over-rotate his body or he will find it difficult to step forward directly in front of his partner. In stepping forward it is better to make no conscious rotation whatsoever, just allowing his body to easily follow the edge round and his body will then correspond with that of his partner, giving the appearance of the two bodies moving as one. Step 15 is a four beat edge for both – right forward outside for the man and left backward outside for the lady.

G

Steps 16, 17, 18 and 19, are known as the promenade steps, which briefly means both are skating facing one another but progressing sideways, the lady to her right and the man to his left. The promenade movement is distinctly Tango although one sometimes sees it used in dance programmes for effect, even though they are not skating to Tango music. The skating of the lobes in the beginning of the Tango, where the man is on the right of the lady, is also very much a Tango position and is known as the 'Outside Tango position'. It will be seen, therefore, that these positions must not be taken too lightly; they are part and parcel of the Tango, the performing of which can either make or mar the dance. The experts will spend much time just in aligning the free legs and bodies so that they match perfectly and move together as if they were joined together.

This is a preferred pattern dance but the majority of the rinks lend themselves to the pattern which is more generally used, as shown in Figs. 12 and 13, pages 101–102. I will now give a little advice on the skating of the promenade steps and the subsequent mohawks following, based on this pattern. I must mention, however, that it is necessary in some rinks to skate the dance almost circular; it is still possible to skate the correct edges but certain edges require to be strengthened while others have to be skated with a slightly lesser curve.

In the aforementioned pattern the lady turns her three, proceeding towards the centre of the rink. Step 15 (right forward outside for the man and left back outside for the lady) is skated boldly, with truly matching free legs. The following promenade edges are also skated with plenty of curve to bring the dancers well round so that they are progressing towards the centre of the rink as they strike on to step 20, the first edge of the mohawk, right forward outside for the lady and left forward inside for the man. It is necessary to strike on to these edges towards the centre of the rink because both the forward and backward edges of the mohawk are four beat edges, and should they strike along the length of the rink, the combined curves of the two edges will bring the dancers too far round, in fact, back on their tracks. Step 21 (left backward outside for the lady, right backward inside for the man) completes the mohawk turn. This mohawk is called a closed swing mohawk because on the first part, the free legs are moved from the back past the tracing foot to the front and back to the heel of the tracing foot for the turn. At the completion of the turn the free legs come off the ice in front of the dancers and are moved from the front again past the tracing foot, behind the dancers and brought back to the heel ready to strike on to step 22.

Do not let the word swing mislead you, the swing of the free leg must be completely controlled but at the same time not giving any appearance of restriction or stiffness. The free legs must move freely but perfectly together just like the pendulum swing of a grandfather clock and what, freely as it moves, could be more controlled than that! I mentioned earlier that I preferred the free leg to move straight through when skating the four beat edges at the beginning of the dance; nobody ever pauses when swinging the free leg through on the swing mohawk and, to my mind, if there is a pause during the four beat edges at the beginning of the dance there should be one when swinging through while skating the mohawk. There are many styles of dancing and differences are bound to occur on some points.

Steps 20 and 21 form the mohawk turn which is a closed swing mohawk. As previously stated, the free leg should swing from the back of the skater to the front and return to the heel of the tracing foot ready to be placed on to the backward edge. The International Skating Union and the National Skating Association of Great Britain ruling for the skating of the closed mohawk is as follows: the free foot is placed on the ice along the outer edge side of the skating foot at the heel. Following the weight transference, the position of the new free foot is in front of the toe of the skating foot. The final closed free hip position gives this the name of closed mohawk.

Care should be taken when placing the new tracing foot on to the ice. It is very common to see dancers swing the free foot round the tracing foot and step back on to it. This partially unbalances the skater and makes an extremely ungainly movement of what should be a simple and very smooth movement. The way to achieve this is to place the new tracing foot on to the ice by the heel of the existing tracing foot and directly beneath the hip, press the existing tracing foot forward until it comes off the ice directly in front of the new tracing foot with the heel in line with the toe. At the completion of the swing through on step 21, the free foot is brought back to the heel to strike on to step 22, for the lady, right forward inside three to right backward outside – six beats – and step 22a for the man, left forward outside, 22b, right forward inside (two one-beat edges which form a chassé) and 22c, left forward outside – four beats – making six beats in all.

The man does his chassé while the lady does her three turn, his four-beat left forward outside edge, step 22c, conforming with the right back outside edge of the lady after her turn. This is the last edge of the dance.

The finer points necessary to give a polished performance will be dealt with in the chapter which deals with the Silver Dance test.

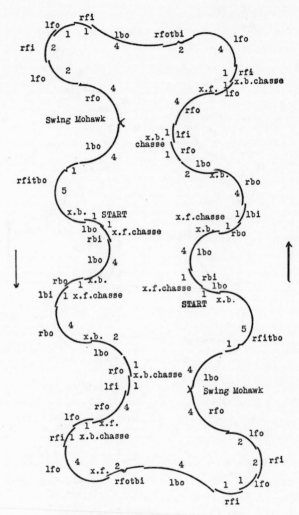

FIG 12 : *The Tango – Lady's steps*

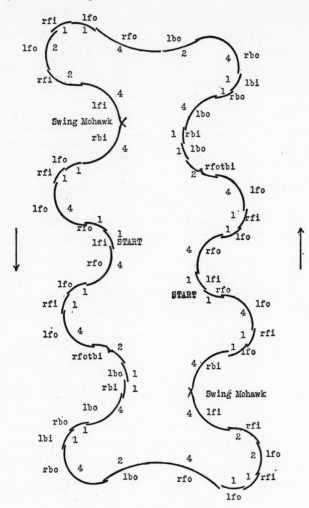

FIG 13 : *The Tango – Man's steps*

The Tango

Edges	Beats	LADY'S STEPS	Step No.	Edges	Beats	MAN'S STEPS
LBO	1	Cross behind	1	RFO	1	Cross-in-front
RBI	1	Cross chassé	2	LFI	1	Cross chassé
LBO	4		3	RFO	4	
RBO	1	Cross behind	4	LFO	1	Cross-in-front
LBI	1	Cross chassé	5	RFI	1	Cross chassé
RBO	4		6	LFO	4	
LBO	2	Cross behind	7	RFOTBI	2	Cross-in-front
RFO	1		8	LBO	1	Cross behind
LFI	1	Cross chassé	9	RBI	1	Cross chassé
RFO	4		10	LBO	4	
LFO	1	Cross-in-front	11	RBO	1	Cross behind
RFI	1	Cross chassé	12	LBI	1	Cross chassé
LFO	4		13	RBO	4	
RFOTBI	2	Cross-in-front	14	LBO	2	Cross behind
LBO	4		15	RFO	4	
RFI	1	Run	16	LFO	1	Run
LFO	1		17	RFI	1	
RFI	2		18	LFO	2	
LFO	2		19	RFI	2	
RFO	4	Closed Mohawk	20	LFI	4	Closed Mohawk
LBO	4		21	RBI	4	
RFI	1	Three turn to	22a	LFO	1	
RBO	5		22b	RFI	1	Chassé
			22c	LFO	4	

CHAPTER SEVENTEEN

The Kilian

Music and Tempo :
March 2/4 at 58 bars per minute
March 4/4 at 29 bars per minute

International Dance

The Kilian appears to be the bane of the average dancer's existence. For some reason best known to themselves, they find it more trouble than any other dance. It has always been a puzzle to me why a dance consisting of fourteen comparatively easy edges should prove to be such a stumbling block. The choctaw is quite difficult but not excessively so if done in the right way. The ability to do a spread is an advantage but not to the extent that some people would like to make it, though the inability to do one serves as a good excuse to the dancer whose aim is to dance really well but without applying the necessary concentration and practice needed to do so. I have even had it suggested to me that it is impossible to do the Kilian choctaw if you are unable to do a spread. In my capacity as a teacher of ice dancing I have proved this to be wrong. It is more difficult but with the co-operation of the pupil it can be done quite well.

It seems to me that the trouble in this dance does not come so much from the inability to do the choctaw as from the psychological effect of having a partner by your side doing the same movement. Apart from this psychological effect, having a partner skating the same edges as you are, by your side, does cause difficulty for the skater whose basic skating movements have been glossed over. For the person who spends sufficient time perfecting the correct pushing action – which is to turn out the pushing foot and push backwards,

NOT to the side, as is so often seen – a considerable amount of the difficulty of skating side by side with a partner will be eliminated.

The edges of both partners MUST run parallel. By pushing straight back, your tracing foot will be driven straight forward, at least ensuring that you both set off in the same direction. This in itself is, of course, not sufficient – accuracy in placing the tracing foot on to the correct edge must be combined with it. The accuracy of the push and the placing of the edge will enable the dancers to move to the left or right in a semi-circular manner with their skates running parallel and not, as is so often seen, in straight lines on forced edges or flats. For those who do not know what a forced edge is, I will explain that an edge is known as a 'forced edge' when the skate is placed on an edge but forced to travel in a straight line, it being natural for an edge to describe a circle. A flat is when both edges are on the ice. This will not curve one way or the other because the outside edge and the inside edge on the same foot oppose one another. There are other factors which make for difficulty in the Kilian hold, such as one or both bending forward, sideways or in extreme cases, backwards.

I have quite often come across dancers who could do the choctaw quite well by themselves but as soon as they are with a partner they do anything but a Kilian choctaw. Very often this is caused by the dancer having tried to do the Kilian without being shown how to link the steps together. This is most important, for in some positions it is impossible to do the choctaw without disastrous results, the lady usually getting too far in front of the man – hence the probability of her doing her choctaw on top of her partner's feet.

The eleventh edge, left backward inside is crossed behind and is often placed down very badly, neither crossed nor otherwise. Accuracy in placing this edge is quite important. By crossing correctly behind it will ensure the foot is placed directly beneath the hip and enable you to do the following backward running steps together more easily.

Another place which seems to catch people badly is that when coming from backward to forward the lady very often steps wide, the two bodies giving the effect of a tripod and completely upsetting the position for starting the dance again. That is why a pair often skate the first sequence of steps reasonably well and then go completely to pieces. Stepping from backward to forward in the Kilian is quite simple if the couple, after crossing the left foot in front of the right (step 13, left back inside), will just turn the right foot to point in the direction of travel and strike from the heel of the left foot without any exaggerated body movement – in fact, just allowing the bodies to follow the movement. See Plates 25 and 26 facing page 96.

It is not necessary to give a diagram of the Kilian as it is done in a circle, with a slight movement out of the circle on the fourth edge, right forward outside and the eighth and ninth edges, right forward outside and left forward inside (crossed behind), after each of which the dancers return to the circle. Although this is a circular dance, the shape is very important. Some dancers completely disregard the shape of the dance, which is a great pity for not only does this make it more difficult to do but, being a fast moving dance, also makes it dangerous, having the same effect as the driver of a car who will cut in. Unfortunately there is no penalty on the ice for this offence.

The first thing to remember when learning the Kilian is that two people cannot do a series of steps, side by side, with one or the other leaning forward from the waist, for this causes a wrench at every movement of the tracing foot. To lean sideways on your partner is equally bad, or to hang on one another for support which will only end up in a tangle on the ice. The hold should be firm but light so as not to influence the movement of your partner. Although I say 'light' I do not mean you should hold so loosely that you concertina apart. That must definitely be avoided and the hold should remain the same throughout the dance.

Speed is very necessary to the character of the dance. A slow moving Kilian is most dull and uninteresting. However, speed should not be gained at the expense of good form as excessive speed leads to bending forward from the waist and a generally untidy performance.

The Kilian is danced to 2/4 or march time and contains two crotchets or four quavers to each bar. Each bar, therefore, contains two strong beats to the bar, on which the dance is based. With the exception of steps three and four, which are skated to two beats of music, all the others are one beat steps as I have shown in the following list of steps:

The Kilian

58 bars per minute of 2/4 tempo
29 bars per minute of 4/4 tempo
The steps are identical for both.

	Edges	*Beats*
1.	LFO	1
2.	Run RFI	1
3.	LFO	2
4.	RFO	2
5.	LFO	1
6.	Run RFI	1
7.	LFO	1
8.	RFO Crossed in front	1
9.	LFI Crossed behind – open choctaw	1
10.	RBO	1
11.	LBI Crossed behind	1
12.	RBO	1
13.	LBI	1
14.	RFI	1

The Hold

The lady's left arm is across the front of the man, the arm held perfectly straight, not bending at the elbow, so that she can be easily steered by the man. The right hand should be firmly placed on the right side of the waist, just above the hip. The man takes the lady's left hand in his left hand, his right arm stretched across the lady's back, and is preferably placed flat on the back of the lady's hand, the thumb holding the palm of her hand. I say flat, because it looks very clumsy when the hands are jumbled together like a bunch of grapes.

Having got the hold right, the lady's left shoulder should be slightly in front of the man's right, the right hip and shoulder of both being back in the first position as for a left forward outside edge. It is a great help if the top half of the body is kept relaxed but controlled, so as to avoid a stiff ungainly movement.

The whole dance should be done with a well defined rise and fall of the tracing knee but, due to the fast tempo of the dance, exaggeration of this should be avoided. The dance in the main being a running movement, the knee action should be of light and undulating character.

You must take care not to change edge on the third edge, left forward outside. Should you do so this will cause you to lurch sideways on to the right forward outside and will end up with the fourth edge becoming a forced edge or straight line in the direction of the barrier. The third edge should maintain its outside edge to the end of the stroke to enable the dancer to stroke straight forward in the same line of travel as the previous edge, on to a true outside edge (4th), which will then curve away from the circle correctly. It is of course equally important that the fifth edge, left forward outside, should be struck in the same line of travel as the fourth. This is done by bringing the feet together at the completion of the fourth edge, turning out the right foot and striking straight back so that the heel of the pushing foot comes off the ice directly in line with the new tracing foot. In other words, by pushing correctly as you should do on to all edges.

Steps 5, 6 and 7 are a repeat of 1, 2 and 3. Care must be taken to turn the pushing foot in on steps 2 and 6 to enable you to push with the outside edge and thereby avoid toe pushing.

We now come to what is one of the most important edges in the Kilian : the eighth edge, right forward outside crossed in front. The reason this is so important is because if you strike a true outside edge, which curves away from the circle, it will automatically place your weight on the right side. By maintaining your weight over the right side this will make it simple to cross your left foot behind on to left forward inside, (the 9th edge), being careful not to move your weight over to the left even the slightest bit. If the weight is maintained in this way you will be able to get the maximum amount of curve, which greatly enhances the movement and puts you in a good position for placing the right foot down on to right backward outside edge, so completing the choctaw.

When placing this tenth edge on to the ice, as it is an open choctaw, it should be placed to the inside of the left foot by the instep. The left foot is run off the ice so that it comes off the ice directly behind the skater, with the heel in line with the heel of the tracing foot, the toe being turned out. As this takes place, the left hip should be strongly checked back to prevent the body swinging round and making the right skate change to an inside edge, which would change the choctaw to a mohawk. Not only would this be wrong but it would mean you would still be travelling out of the circle, when, in fact, it is at this point that the dancers move back on to the circle.

The eleventh edge, left backward inside, is crossed behind and, I must add, this crossing step is often very badly performed. The left foot should be tucked in neatly behind and beside the right foot. It will then be directly beneath the left hip and will make it easy for you to place the twelfth edge, right backward outside, close by the side of the left foot, as it should be. The eleventh edge is crossed behind at the completion of the choctaw. As the bodies are moved slightly clockwise, or to the right, facing slightly into the circle, care must be taken not to over rotate the bodies or the following edge, right back outside, will tend to become an inside – and subsequently the thirteenth edge, left backward inside, crossed in front, will have the same tendency to become an outside. When this happens, as so often does, it will be very difficult indeed to step forward on to the fourteenth edge – right forward inside edge. The man will be in such a position that he will have to step over his partner's pushing foot causing a nasty lurch forward. The lady is often at fault here by stepping wide on to the fourteenth edge, right forward inside.

Always endeavour to come forward without an exaggerated movement. On this edge the bodies rotate ready for the commencement again, so that they are facing slightly out of the circle; this is most important but must not be overdone. Neglect to move the bodies round into the starting position leads to a very scrappy start to the new sequence, the dancers running straight into the circle instead of round the circle. From there on trouble is in store. This is the prime reason why so often the first sequence of the dance is performed quite well and the following sequences very poorly.

CHAPTER EIGHTEEN

The Blues

Tempo : Blues 4/4 and 22 bars per minute

International Dance

Preferred pattern

The Blues is skated to slow music, twenty-two bars per minute. A few years ago the Tango used to be danced at exactly the same tempo (until the four beat edges came into being in the first part of the Tango). In spite of this, how-ever, the rhythms of the two dances bear no resemblance to each other, the Blues being much smoother. When I say the Blues is smoother than the Tango I do not mean the Blues is a better dance than the Tango, for this is not the case. All I intend to convey is that they are very different in character and movement. The Tango is more a staccato or abrupt rhythm, while the Blues is an adagio – or, one might even say, lazy – rhythm but nevertheless a very attractive one. Be-cause this dance has a leisurely rhythm it does not mean that you must not travel fast. Actually a certain amount of speed greatly enhances the appearance of the dance, giving greater length to the four beat edges. Naturally you would not travel as fast as you would for the Fourteen-step or Kilian, or the whole character of the dance would be lost. Were we to travel at the same speed in each dance, regardless of its own special character, it would be rather pointless having different rhythms and tempi in order to vary the dances and break the monotony of doing the same dance throughout the interval.

Although the Tango and Blues are unlike in rhythm there is a similarity of steps in certain parts of the dance. The first five steps for the lady are the same, thus causing a little con-

111

fusion for the man when he first learns the dance. Here, however, the similarity ends.

In the Blues you cannot pay too much attention to the rise and fall of the tracing knee, the whole movement of the dance being affected by it. A good rise and fall of the knee keeps the long edges flowing and prevents loss of speed. At the same time it is essential that the rise and fall is not jerky, just slowly bending and straightening over the course of the edge so that at no time is the knee stationary in the bent or straight position. The free leg must be slowly moving in conjunction with the tracing knee. It is very common to see couples dancing on permanently bent knees, giving no rise and fall whatsoever. It is most important that the tracing knee straightens to allow the dancers to stroke on to the next edge with both knees straight, enabling them to slowly bend while making the stroke. Without this there cannot be any rise and fall. A good movement to practise in order to attain a good rise and fall, is to bend the knee on the count of one, rising on the count of two and, if it is a four beat edge, sinking again on the count of three and rising on the count of four, synchronising the movement of the free leg to match.

The first spot of bother usually arises at the man's fourth edge, left forward outside, three turn back inside. The trouble here can be caused either by the lady or the man. If the lady pulls her back edges, 4 and 5, (or as officially listed by the National Skating Association as 4a, right backward outside crossed behind and 4b, left backward inside crossed in front) round too sharply, she will pull away from the man, making it difficult for him to do his three and cause considerable gaping at this point. On the other hand the man must strike to the left of his partner for his three, for if he strikes at his partner he will be in a bad position for the right backward outside. However, he must take care not to strike wide of his partner or this will have the same effect as the lady pulling her edges round.

Plate 30 An unimpressive start (Chapter 20, page 124)

Plate 31 An impressive start (Chapter 20, page 124)

The following edges are the same for the lady as for the man. The fifth edge, right backward outside, must be skated with a good strong easy curve, but not too sharp or the following left forward outside will take you too far across the centre. Care must be taken at this point not to rotate the bodies or considerable difficulty will ensue in striking truly on to the next left forward outside edge. As the man turns his three the hold is changed from the closed or Waltz hold to the open or Foxtrot hold, the latter hold being maintained to the end of the dance. It will be seen, therefore, that the man's right hip is next to his partner's left hip, the man's left side being forward and the lady's right side forward. Should either try to make a rotation it would be impossible to maintain this position. The strike from backward to forward is made by dropping the free foot to the instep of the skating foot and stroking sideways on to the forward edge. This way you will get a true curve on the new edge which will eventually bring you round to face in the opposite direction.

REMEMBER, there are no straight lines in skating, unless specified. I say, unless specified, because there are certain dances where a series of flats are used for effect purposes, for instance in the Paso Doble, which will be dealt with in another volume. As the lady is on the inside of the circle when skating her fifth edge, she must take the depth of edge from her partner, remembering that he has to come round her. This is another reason for not rotating the bodies when stepping from backward to forward.

When the left forward outside edge is taken too far round, there is a strong tendency to get out of the awkward position in which it places you, by omitting to cross-roll the following right forward outside edge, causing a change of edge on the left foot. So by pulling the right backward outside edge (fifth edge) round too sharply you find it upsets the run of the following three or four edges. The next edge, right forward outside (cross-roll) step 6, should be skated very full

H

and strong, with a bold sweeping curve which brings you round to face the barrier; this enables you to strike towards the barrier with the two-beat left forward outside, making it possible for the next three edges to be skated strongly without bringing you too far across the rink. The first two of these edges are run, right forward inside and left forward outside. This is an unusual run because it begins with an inside edge. The third of these edges, step 11, is right forward inside and is very often done on the flat or even on an outside edge. You should be very particular to avoid this, since if an outside edge is skated instead of an inside edge, it comes round in the wrong direction and places the body in a bad position for the twelfth edge, the left forward inside edge of the choctaw. This inaccuracy is usually caused by pulling badly into the circle while skating steps 8, 9 and 10, and not running correctly.

When stroking on to the twelfth edge, left forward inside, the first edge of the closed choctaw, particular care should be taken to ensure it starts off in the same line as the previous edge. Often dancers strike almost at right angles to the previous edge, causing the bodies to lean over to the left and most certainly leading to a very poor left forward inside edge. It also makes it difficult to place truly on to the second edge of the choctaw, right backward outside. Careful observation of average dancers will show that more often than not this edge starts off on an inside edge which, of course, turns it into a mohawk – which is *not* the prescribed turn. The left forward inside edge of the choctaw should be skated boldly with a strong curve, but not exaggerated, with a strong check of the left hip and shoulder as the right back outside edge is placed down. Care must be taken here to see that the left foot does not come off the ice and swing across the right leg – should this happen it will be difficult to check the left hip. When the right back outside is placed on the ice, the left free leg should come off the ice slightly

to the outside of the tracing foot, and not be allowed to
swing across the tracing foot. Otherwise it will tend to bring
the left hip and shoulder forward. I emphasise this because
it is such a common fault. When control is lost on this edge,
it usually ends up on an inside, from which it is almost
impossible to cross behind for the long left backward outside. The result is an awkward attempt to do so with the
couple bending badly forward at the waist in the effort, and
nearly always falling off the four-beat left back outside edge
long before the four beats are up.

It should now be thoroughly understood that the choctaw
must be strong and well controlled so that the back outside
edge is clean and not a change of edge. However, although
the edges should be strong, the depth of curve on the forward
and backward edges should be equal.

A very good method of practising the choctaw is to try
to hold the left forward inside edge for a complete circle with
the left hip and shoulder forward, the body perfectly erect.
Place the right back outside down, and try to hold for a
complete circle or for as long as your speed lasts. When you
can do a good choctaw on your own comfortably, you will
find that with little practice it is quite easy to perform with a
partner.

While skating step 14, left backward outside, (cross-roll)
of four beats duration, I must emphasise the necessity for
not rotating the bodies. The correct placing of the edge, the
flexing of the tracing knee and the correct body weight will
give you the depth of curve you require. Should you try to
rotate this edge, *as is so often done*, a ghastly position will
result and the couple will lurch forward on to the fifteenth
edge, right forward inside, bent forward at the waist. More
often than not they will land on an outside rather than an
inside. It is most important to strike an inside edge here because it is the beginning of the sweeping curve formed by
the remaining edges of the dance.

Assuming you have struck correctly on to the inside edge on step 15, take care to strike straight on in the same line of travel as the previous edge for the lady's sixteenth edge, left forward outside three, and the man's step 16, (a) and (b), left forward outside chassé, to allow the last edge, step 17, left forward outside for the man and right backward outside

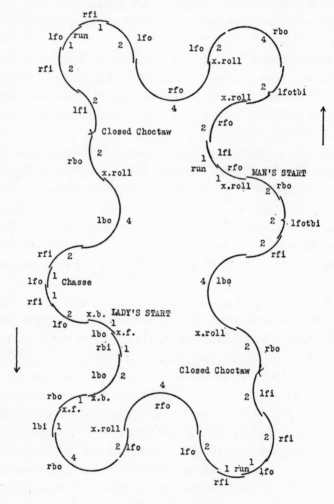

FIG 14 : *The Blues*

for the lady, to be skated on a strong curve without coming back on your tracks – thereby completing a very attractive boldly skated lobe commencing with step 15 and ending with step 17. So we arrive at the end of the first sequence, correctly positioned for the commencement of the next sequence.

Blues

Edges	Beats	LADY'S STEPS	Step No.	Edges	Beats	MAN'S STEPS
LBO	1	Cross behind	1	RFO	1	Cross roll
RBI	1	Cross-in-front	2	LFI	1	Run
LBO	2		3	RFO	2	
RBO	1	Cross behind	4–4a	LFOTBI	2	
LBI	1	Cross-in-front	4b			
RBO	4		5	RBO	4	
LFO	2		6	LFO	2	
RFO	4	Cross roll	7	RFO	4	Cross roll
LFO	2		8	LFO	2	
RFI	1	Run	9	RFI	1	Run
LFO	1		10	LFO	1	
RFI	2		11	RFI	2	
LFI	2	Closed choctaw	12	LFI	2	
RBO	2		13	RBO	2	
LBO	4	Cross roll	14	LBO	4	Cross roll
RFI	2		15	RFI	2	
LFO	1	Three turn to	16a	LFO	1	
LBI	1		16b	RFI	1	Chassé
RBO	2		17	LFO	2	

CHAPTER NINETEEN

Pair Dancing

Music of own choice – strict tempo

Pair dancing in relation to dancing is, one might say, as free skating in relation to figure skating. Therefore it is not the least interesting branch of dancing, provided you are able to demonstrate your ability by making up a programme of different steps, short spirals, pirouettes etc., forming an original programme.

The duration of a pair dance programme in the Silver dance test is three minutes. In competitions, however, the length varies according to the rules of the competition. Your aim should be to make up a really original programme. Although it is essential to have originality, do not think that this is the only thing that matters in pair dancing. A step is not always good because it is original, there being many ways in which it could be unsuitable. For instance it might considerably cramp the flow which is so necessary to dancing, and in pair dancing any step which tends to check the flow or reduce the speed is no use. As in free skating, you must cover the ice with plenty of dash and movement. On the other hand the step might be artistically bad and then once again it becomes of little use. Not only must a programme be original but it must be artistic and pleasing to the eye.

In setting out to build a programme there are all manner of things to be taken into account, such as using the entire ice surface. A programme never looks good if performed just at one end or part of the rink, nor if it continually goes round and round the rink in the same direction. When a programme is being judged, rink craft, or the correct and full use of the ice surface, is taken into account and will have some bearing on the mark given.

When building a programme you must first try to have some kind of geographical plan in your mind. The procedure in building a pair dancing programme is in many respects similar to that of building a house. The first step in building a house is to choose a piece of land in a place you like, making sure you are not going to become tired of it in a short time; likewise the dancer chooses a piece of music or, in some instances, two or three pieces of music which will join together to make a programme of the required length, making sure he is not going to become tired of it in a short time, and bearing in mind he is going to have to listen to it many times and often for quite a lengthy period. Like the builder, the dancer then lays the foundation, which is the pattern he has in mind for covering the ice surface in the most interesting manner possible.

When this is done, you are now ready to start building the programme. Listen carefully to the music and try to let the music suggest various movements. In this way you use the music to the best advantage and, in many instances, it will lead to originality. While doing this you must have the character of the music uppermost in your mind. The programme is now like a building in its rough state and has to have the refinements put into it. This the dancer does by practice, and having practised the programme sufficiently well, movements, which at first seemed difficult, will now be easy. Many improvements will suggest themselves and so you go on polishing the programme until you arrive at the finished product.

We have now arrived at the final stage: the programme is built and practised and there is but one thing left to make it as attractive as possible. This is to make sure the free legs are well turned out, with the toes pointed and perfectly matching when moving, adding arm movements where they are likely to enhance the programme but at all times avoiding any exaggerated movement which is likely to stand out as something having happened, instead of blending with the whole and generally improving the general picture.

Planning in this manner will enable you to produce the best possible programme with the steps and movements in keeping with the music and pleasing to the eye. If, when watching a programme, you get the feeling it is going on forever then it is not a very good one. On the other hand if the programme has so held your interest that you are surprised when it is over, it must have been pleasing to the eye and have genuinely held your interest. This would be a first-rate programme. See Plates 27, 28 and 29 facing pages 97 and 112.

While the dancer is given, to a great extent, a free hand in the selection of the steps and movements he wishes to incorporate into the programme, there are certain rules by which he must abide:

First: Jumps and lifts are not allowed.

Second: Most free skating movements are permissible with the following limitations:

Spirals or pivots must not exceed in length 3 measures of Waltz or 2 measures of 4/4 or 6/8 tempo.

Spins must not exceed 3 revolutions.

Changes of hold are permissible and should be used to enhance the programme. Separations are allowed to change position but if separations are used, care must be taken not to be apart for more than four measures of Waltz – three beats to the bar – or two measures of other tempi – 4/4, 6/8 etc.

Skating on the toes should not be used to excess.

In recent years we have seen many programmes which do not conform strictly to these rules, many having semi-lifts and quite excessive use of the toes. This tends to make many dancers take the attitude: 'if they can do it so can I.' My advice here is, if you decide to break the rules, do not be disappointed if you are marked down for doing so. The fact that you have seen a couple receive very good marks while breaking these rules has no bearing on your case. Probably the couple you saw were extremely good and therefore managed to get very good marks in spite of taking this liberty; more than likely had they not taken this liberty their mark would have been half a mark higher. The moral is, if you must break the rules wait until you are a champion before doing so, or you may remain a very disappointed person for evermore. Learn to do a real skating programme. After all, hopping around on the toes is not skating!

As from 1st September 1968 the Regulations for Free Dancing have been amended and read as follows:

'Free dancing, does not have to have a required sequence of steps, but shall consist of a non-repetitive combination of new or known dance movements, displayed according to the dancers' own ideas and arrangement. Its purpose is to test the competitors' general dancing knowledge and ability as well as their originality and inventiveness.

'The timing begins as soon as the couple begin to dance.

'Couples may choose their own music but it must consist of dance music with a tempo, rhythm and character suitable for ice dancing. A combination of two or more tunes is permitted provided that there is no break or discontinuity of the music.

'All the recognised steps, turns, changes of position are permissible, as well as certain free skating movements which accord with the rhythm and music and are in keeping with the character of the dances. Feats of strength and skating skill, which do not form part of the dance sequence, but are inserted to show physical prowess, shall be counted against the competitors using them.

'Certain free skating movements, such as some spins, brief arabesques or pivots, and separations to accomplish changes of position, jumps and lifting of the lady are permitted in ice dancing when used with the following limitations:

(a) Separation of partners for steps, arabesques, pivots, etc., are permitted providing the separation is no more than outstretched arms length for a duration of five seconds. During the end sequence of this dance a parting of up to eight seconds is permitted.

(b) Arabesques and pivots may not exceed the longer movements of the Compulsory Dances, i.e. 4 bars Waltz time (3/4) or 2 bars of other music (4/4 or 6/8).

(c) Spins (Pirouettes) must not exceed 3 revolutions.

(d) Skating on toe picks shall not be done to an excess.

(e) Short, jerky movements are acceptable only when they fit the character of the music. In general, smooth running edges are preferred.

(f) Stops in which couples are stationary on the ice surface whilst body movements, twisting and posing take place must not exceed two bars of music.

(g) Small dance lifts up to a maximum of $1\frac{1}{2}$ turns, in which the gentleman must not riase his hands higher than his waistline are permitted, provided they fit in with the character of the music, or emphasise certain passages of the music.

(h) Small low jumps which serve to change direction or the step of one partner are permitted, provided they only take up a half turn and are carried out in a dancing position or at the most at one arms length. Both partners are not allowed to jump at the same time.'

CHAPTER TWENTY

The Silver Dance Test

For the benefit of those who wish to have proof of their ability to dance well, I intend to explain what is required of them to pass the Silver Dance Test.

Having been through the elementary stages of dancing, a more polished display is expected of you. The fact that you are able to do all the dances accurately, that is to say without any technical mistakes, is not enough; you must really express the spirit of dancing. Where in a Bronze test you might scrape through with mediocre rhythm and a not too easy movement, you must now display a strong flowing movement with plenty of rhythm; in other words, to do a series of steps with a band playing in the background is not adequate. Although I have gone to some length to explain that there is a big difference between the Bronze and Silver standard, do not be discouraged by this. It does not mean you have to be perfect – if that were the case there would be no necessity for the higher tests.

When dancing your Silver test pay particular attention to your carriage. There is no more ungainly sight than to see a couple dancing with bad deportment; the whole effect is lost, no matter how perfect their footwork and technique generally. Start at the beginning of the dance with good deportment and maintain it throughout the dance. When starting, take up your position at the part of the rink where you intend to begin the dance. This might seem an obvious thing to do but there are occasions when you see a couple amble on to the ice and when the music starts they find they have not placed themselves in that part of the rink which will allow them to commence the dance correctly.

The usual way to start most dances is to stand side by side, the lady holding the man's right hand with her left. Stand perfectly upright but not stiff and wait for a few bars of music to be played before attempting to move off, in order to feel the rhythm before doing so. Four bars being a phase of music, this is an admirable time to wait without being long enough to make you feel awkward. It is usual, however, for the organist or band to play a two or four bar introduction. Make sure you start on the first beat in the bar, as dancing on the weak beat detracts from the general performance. While waiting for the music to start, try to look confident; the psychological effect is good. See Plates 30 and 31 facing page 113.

If you are nervous, as most people are to some extent, try not to show it. Remember it is not sympathy you require, it is marks; if you look nervous the onlookers, instead of seeing the best in you, start off expecting to be sorry for you. You don't want that! If you can command their interest from the beginning and retain it through the test then you have that little something that is so necessary to good dancing. Of course, not everyone has that mysterious little something, but if you start by trying to develop it you are on the right road to success and it will stand you in good stead later on when you are more experienced and decide to try for your Gold.

To carry out the above instructions with regard to confidence, it must be apparent to you that you cannot dance a test with confidence if you are not well up to the standard. It is all too common at the present time for pupils to be pushing to go in for a test when they are very much on the borderline or even below the required standard. Occasionally they get through but more often they fail and are consequently very disappointed. When this happens you often hear them say 'so and so passed and I am better than her' or 'that judge doesn't like me. She always marks me down.' Believe me, the judges are not trying to fail you, and if you go in for a test before you are ready you have no one to blame but yourself. I hope you will believe me when I tell you that just to be up to the standard is not sufficient for the average person. You must remember that dancing in a test is not like dancing in a dance interval; you have three judges to face and often quite a gallery of spectators. You want to be at least twenty-five per cent above the standard, and of course the more you are above, the greater it adds to your comfort. Always take the advice of your instructor as to when you are ready to go in. He has studied your dancing and your capacity for nerves, therefore he is in an excellent position to judge your chances of passing.

A great many dancers are inclined to disregard this advice, possibly imagining the instructor is purposely holding them back. You can take it from me that he would not do that; his pupils' interests are his interests and he is just as keen as the pupil that they should get through as soon as possible. If, however, he is at all conscientious he cannot allow his pupil to waste his or her money by going in before there is a good chance of passing. Apart from that, there is nothing so disappointing as to fail a hard-worked-for test. Then, there are the pupils who become bored with practising something they have become reasonably good at, when they are within striking distance of their test. There is really no necessity for this, for they can always carry on with the next stage.

It is sometimes very difficult for pupils when they have become quite good. People keep telling them how they have improved just recently and ask : 'When are you going in for your test? You will pass easily' and so on, such remarks usually coming from those who know very little about dancing. All this makes it very difficult for them to imagine that nerves can play such a large part and bring them down below the pass mark. This makes it very trying for the instructor who, from experience, knows more or less how much to allow in your individual case for the great enemy of tests — NERVES.

It is not uncommon to hear people say how unfair the judging is. I wonder how many of these critics of judging ever stop to think what a difficult and thankless job these judges really have. They give their time voluntarily to the cause of skating. Their job should, and would, be a happy one if dancers would only do that little bit extra before attempting their test; it must be very upsetting for them to have to keep failing people when all the time they know those they failed think they should have passed.

The Silver Dance test consists of :

The American Waltz	tempo	66
Tango	"	27
Kilian	"	29/58
Blues	"	22

3 minutes Pair Dancing.

The candidate has also to dance one of the dances solo, the dance to be selected by the judges. The solo dance is not marked but if in the judges' opinion the candidate is not capable of dancing to the required standard without the assistance of a partner, the candidate could be failed. The judges also have the power to request the candidate to dance with another partner should they feel he is getting too much assistance.

Candidates must pass on each of the compulsory dances before they are allowed to do the Pair Dancing. If, in the opinion of the judges, the candidate is probably worthy of passing, they may, at their discretion, allow the candidate to re-skate not more than two of the dances. It is possible to have a re-skate of the Pair Dancing but only in exceptional circumstances.

I would like to quote the following paragraph from the Handbook of the National Skating Association of Great Britain :

'It should be emphasised that strict observance of time and academic correctness in skating the steps of the dances are NOT IN THEMSELVES SUFFICIENT to gain a pass mark. In addition a candidate is required to move really well and to give character and life to a dance. In the free dancing, CARRIAGE AND MOVEMENT WILL BE CONSIDERED OF PARAMOUNT IMPORTANCE and marked accordingly. A difficult programme is not essential – a simple one well performed, will carry more marks than an ambitious one poorly executed.'

There are many people who bemoan their fate at having to do a dance on their own. I think it is a very good idea, but then I ought to. When I first started to teach ice dancing it was unheard of to expect pupils to dance on their own but I insisted on all my pupils doing each of the dances equally well on their own before I would consent to their going in for their test, hence failures were very rare and the standard of the dancing very high. You must remember that it IS a test of the individual NOT of a pair, and by insisting on the candidate doing a dance on his or her own, it once and for all dispels any doubt in the mind of the judge as to whether the candidate is being held up by his or her partner. After all, you would not attempt to do a Silver figure test if you could not do the figures and free skating quite surely on your own. This is the equivalent standard, only in dancing, so surely it is not asking much of you to expect you to able to do the dances on your own?

There are those who think it is much more difficult to pass a test today than it used to be; they think the standard is that much higher. This is not the case. In my opinion, as far as the compulsory dances are concerned, it is certainly no higher, if anything the opposite. The reason why there are probably more failures today is because people are in too much of a hurry – they want to skip the basics and have a go.

In other words they want to run before they can walk. *The first moves are the most important in anything we do.*

A few final hints :

THE AMERICAN WALTZ. When waltzing in a test there is a strong tendency to lean forward. I say in a test, not because the tendency is not there at other times, but because it is more so in a test, being very often caused by dancing on too stiff knees. Dancing requires really flexible knees and upright carriage so as to allow the edge to run round easily. Just for once the lady follows the man blindly. And a little advice for the man : Keep your eyes open to see that you do not deviate from pattern and to enable you, should you do so, to recognise the fault and rectify it.

TANGO. Avoid double tracking and toe pushing. Allow the shoulders and hips to rotate evenly. Keep your free legs moving together.

KILIAN. Once more a strong flexible knee action is necessary. Try to have a nice light airy movement so that your feet appear to be skimming over the ice.

BLUES. Lots of rhythm, easy knee movement. Keep free legs the same height and, above all, do not allow your free leg to swing through at a different time to that of your partner, which is a fault very prominent in most dances.

PAIR DANCING. Move in unison, keep a good speed and do not cramp it. Continuity and co-ordination are most essential.

CHAPTER TWENTY-ONE

Common Faults to avoid in a Test

When dancing in a test you will find faults crop up which
would not normally happen in an ordinary dance interval.
The cause of this is usually nerves, and it is therefore impossible to emphasise too strongly the necessity for being a
little above the standard before attempting to demonstrate
your ability before the judges.

The most prominent of these unforeseen faults is to stiffen
up, giving a very lifeless effect, with complete lack of movement. By stiffening up, I do not mean just a lack of movement, but a stiffening of the whole body. Body rhythm is
most essential to dancing and it can only be acquired by
perfect relaxation. It is not uncommon to see a dancer whose
body is completely rigid but at the same time has quite a
reasonable rise and fall of the knee, giving the appearance
of inexperience and something missing. Even so, this is preferable to being completely devoid of movement, and it is only
in cases where the dancer normally has a really strong knee
action that he retains it in a test, due to nervous tension. I
mention this because anyone worthwhile has a certain amount
of nervous apprehension when performing before judges. This
is a natural reaction which shows you have something to
give. The best of skaters have it but they control it.

Another thing to avoid in a test is looking as though you
thought the judges were going to eat you. Look as though
you enjoy dancing and smile, for it is amazing how this
improves the appearance of a dancer. It is very difficult to
remain tense and smile; smiling is the easiest way of re-
laxing, so try it. Picture a dancer with a long face and
another who is smiling and you will find it gives you more
pleasure to watch the latter. The judges have feelings as well

as you and naturally will be more disposed to give good marks to the person who gives them pleasure to watch and does not show a feeling of uncertainty. Of course you might say, 'the judges are judging my dancing, not my appearance.' So they are, but you must remember they are human beings, not machines, and if you look as though you enjoy it, this must have the psychological effect of preparing them to see the best in you. After all, dancing is supposed to be pleasing to watch and if you make your exhibition attractive the more marks you will gain.

Avoid starting off in an uncertain manner. Wait for the music and start off together. It is a good plan to arrange beforehand how many bars you are going to wait so that there is no uncertainty in either of your minds as to when you are going to strike off. An uncertain beginning not only looks bad but very often upsets the complete run of the dance, which may be your best. It is most disconcerting if you go wrong early on in the test, all through paying insufficient attention to the start.

When dancing, freedom of movement is essential, so allow your edges to run easily but strongly round. You often see a dancer trying to strengthen the curve by pulling on his or her partner and this should be avoided at all costs, for instead of strengthening the curve it merely upsets the run of the dance. This makes it very difficult for your partner and, what is even worse, causes both of you to lean forward badly from the waist and the free legs to swing round in an uncertain way, the whole thing looking completely out of control.

On no account allow yourself to look at your feet. It gives the judges the impression that you do not know what your feet are doing, and in a Silver test there are judges who would fail a person for doing so, in my opinion quite rightly. Invariably, if you look down, the shoulders come forward a little giving a hump-backed effect, ruining the deportment and so the appearance of the dance is lost and the Silver medal is lost as well. To fail in this way is particularly disappointing as you have probably worked very hard for the test. This is a bad habit which can be easily overcome by always looking where you are going when dancing in the dance intervals. It is impossible to look at your feet and see the other couples who are dancing immediately in front or to the side of you.

Make sure your rise and fall of the knee is in unison with your partner's otherwise the effect will be two heads bobbing up and down, ruining the rhythm and giving an ungainly look to the dance.

The rotation of the shoulders and hips must be even so that, when in the Waltz hold, the shoulders are at all times parallel with those of your partner. Never have one shoulder nearer to your partner than the other, and in dances where the shoulders rotate into different positions this must be done evenly so as to give the desired effect.

When coming together in readiness for the start of the dance, see that you hold correctly from the beginning; to keep changing the hold or moving the hands during the dance looks bad and will lose you marks. Keep the fingers together not spread out and, in the Kilian particularly, do not have the hands bunched together, but keep them flat. Always make the hands as inconspicuous as possible.

CHAPTER TWENTY-TWO

Summary of the Intermediate First Class Gold, First Class Gold, and Competitive Dancing

As indicated in the Introduction, I hope to deal fully with these tests in a subsequent volume. Briefly they consist of the following:

Intermediate gold dance test

The compulsory dances in this test are:

(1) Starlight Waltz

(2) Rhumba (Gregory)

(3) European Waltz

(4) Silver Samba

(5) Original Set Dance

The minimum pass mark required for each dance in this test is 3.8, but in order to pass the test the candidate must have an aggregate of 21.0 marks which is an average of 4.2 for each dance. Should you dance one dance to the minimum of 3.8 you can still pass but this will mean you will have to dance the remaining four dances to 4.3. If you have two dances down to the minimum the remaining dances will have to be danced to 4.66 or, near enough 4.5 and as 4.5 is the pass mark for the Gold Dance test you will see that to have two dances down to the minimum means you make it necessary to dance the remaining three to Gold standard, which is asking a lot. It is never wise, therefore, to attempt a test unless you have every dance up to the required standard. There is no free dancing in the Intermediate Gold Dance Test.

First class or gold dance test

The compulsory dances in this test are:

(1) Argentine Tango

(2) Westminster Waltz

(3) Quickstep

(4) Viennese Waltz

(5) Paso Doble

(6) Original Set Dance

The minimum pass mark for each dance is 4.0.

The minimum total marks – 27. I will not go into detail over this because I am sure you can work it out for yourself in the same way I did for the previous test.

Free dancing of 3½ minutes duration

Some years ago the N.S.A. Gold Dance test used to have a 1½ minute Exhibition Dance of your own composition. The Intermediate-Gold Dance test and the Gold Dance test have now an Original Set Dance of the competitors own composition, this is to some extent reverting back but there is a difference however. Whereas in the Exhibition Dance you could move over the ice at will, in the Original Set Dance you have to dance round the perimeter without crossing over the centre line of the rink.

As from 1st September 1968 the Original Set Dance will be introduced Internationally. I will therefore give a list of rules which must be observed :

(1) This dance must not be a free dance.

(2) Each couple may choose their own music and tempo.

(3) Only regular dance rhythms with constant tempo may be used.

(4) The choice of steps, connecting steps, turns and rotations is free, provided they conform to the rules of the I.S.U.

(5) Separation of partners must not exceed the duration of one bar of music.

(6) Toe steps are not permitted.

(7) Hand-in-hand positions with outstretched arms are

not permitted except at the start of the sequence and must not exceed seven steps.

(8) This dance must be composed of repetitive sequences. The sequences must consist either of a half or a whole circuit.

(9) Reverse direction is permitted provided it is constant.

(10) The dance sequence must not cross the midline of the rink.

(11) It is permitted to change the dancing hold three times in each sequence, if this takes a half circuit. If it takes a full circuit, six changes are permitted.

In marking the Original Set Dance, the following points are observed :

(1) Correct timing of the dance to the music.

(2) The movement of the dancers in rhythm with the music and the relation of this movement to the character of the music.

(3) The composition (difficulty and variety) of the dance.

(4) The placement of the steps of the dances on the ice surface.

(5) Clearness and sureness.

(6) The style of the dance couples as shown by their carriage, form and unison.

There are many dancers who prefer not to dance in competitions. The reason they usually give is that they dance solely for pleasure and do not wish to make a business of it. Competition dancing may seem like a business to some, and having to pay so much attention to the finer points is not their idea of pleasure. To the really keen dancers, though, competition dancing gives them the opportunity of testing their skill against others and they can judge for themselves, by the position in which they finish, how their dancing is progressing. This keeps their interest at concert pitch throughout the season and allows for the maximum amount of improvement to be made. The adding of the finer points is not a business to them but a source of getting a great deal of pleasure from their dancing. Every point gained gives great satisfaction and however hard it has been to attain, the result is surely worth the effort.

If the dancers who dance for pleasure and do not like making a business of it would only give up one or two weeks to practising the rudiments, they would find after a time they enjoy their dancing far more than before. Another point very much in favour of improving your dancing is that it widens your range of partners. If you are a man and a poor dancer, you would think twice before asking a lady of Silver medal standard to dance with you; unless of course you happened to be one of those happy people who seem blissfully ignorant of their inability to dance well. However good the lady is, it is very difficult for her to control a dancer who swings her all over the rink and very often at a speed far in excess of his ability. Therefore a little thought must make it quite apparent to the dancer who dances for pleasure that although he might get a certain amount of pleasure from dancing with a girl who is far better than himself, it is just hard work for the girl.

By this do not think that I mean the good girl dancer does not care to dance with anyone not as good as herself, far from it; the average girl is only too pleased to dance with anyone who wishes to improve and will very often help them considerably, particularly as there are far more good girl dancers than men and they are usually only too pleased to encourage them. You might say 'Why are there more good girl dancers than men?' I would say there are two reasons; firstly, girls usually have more time than men and secondly, very often having fewer responsibilities, are better able to afford tuition. This is not always the case as many girls are at business all day and do their practice in the evening, the same as the average man has to do, but in my experience I find where girls score over men is that if they become very interested they will go without other things in order to have regular lessons, or a regular lesson, and there are very few men who will do this.

Dancing must essentially be graceful and it is more natural for girls to be so, on the ice, without feeling self-conscious. I also find that most girls, having made up their minds that they want to dance really well, will apply extraordinary patience and work hard until they have reached the standard they set themselves. Most men aim to be essentially manly and in no way to resemble the fairer sex; they have a horror of looking foolish. This makes it very difficult for them in the early stages of their dancing career to practise the graceful movements necessary to ice dancing, and they are liable to become very self-conscious, feeling sure that everyone is watching them make a foolish exhibition of themselves. Consequently they are liable to do far less practice than is essential. Of course after a while they get over this and realise that they look neither girlish nor foolish and that the positions they practise are necessary to be able to skate. Even so I find that it is rare for men to have as much patience or work as hard as girls.

For those who wish to go in for competitive dancing I would suggest that they start off by entering one of the minor competitions first, such as a 'novices' or a 'drawn partner' competition. Even though you may be a very good dancer it will give you the opportunity of finding out what kind of tricks your nerves play on you – and they can play some very funny ones indeed! It also gives you the opportunity of being quite possibly among the first four or five in your first competition which is very encouraging. Some of these competitions have quite a high standard and perhaps a number of dancers entered who have just failed to win a prize in higher class competitions and are therefore still eligible to compete.

Until you have entered a few competitions and become

accustomed to dancing in front of judges, and possibly a fair-sized audience, it is quite impossible to tell what your prospects are of becoming a good competition dancer. There are some really good dancers who can never produce their true standard when dancing in competition and a minority who always dance their best when competing against others.

The more nervous you are the more competitive events you ought to enter. Each time you will become more accustomed to dancing in front of judges, but do not allow yourself to become disheartened if you fail to win often. Learn to smile at your failures just as you would at your successes.

I hope you have found this book of considerable instructional value and wish you the best of luck in your ice dancing.

CHAPTER TWENTY-THREE

Six Golden Rules for Ice Dancing

1. Always push correctly from the edge of the skate, not the toe.
2. Keep perfectly in time with the music.
3. Maintain perfect continuity throughout.
4. Maintain a smooth rise and fall of the tracing knee throughout.
5. Carry yourself with good deportment.
6. Make sure your free leg is well turned out and the toe pointed.

Analysis of the above rules

1. You can be said to have pushed correctly (a) when the heel of your pushing foot comes off the ice directly in line with the heel of the tracing foot when you are going forward, with the tracing skate proceeding straight forward in the same line as the previous edge, and (b) when the heel of the pushing foot comes off the ice directly in front of the toe of the tracing foot when progressing backwards, again with the tracing skate proceeding in the same line as the previous edge.

2. It is not sufficient to put your foot down on the correct beat; this in itself is only partially keeping time. Every movement you make should blend into the timing of the music.

3. What is continuity of movement? Continuous movement, performed in a rhythmical manner so that there is no apparent break in the flow when moving from one foot to the other. Moving the free leg and tracing knee in time with the music in a similar manner to a conductor's baton when conducting an orchestra. Making rotations of the body

138

smoothly and easily in time with the music so that it flows from one movement to the next.

4. It is only possible to make a smooth rise and fall if the knees are straight at the beginning of the push which will allow the tracing knee to sink gradually throughout the push. It follows that the knees should always be straight when the feet are together, this being the rise.

5. You may be said to have perfect deportment if your body is perfectly erect but relaxed, with the head up, NOT LOOKING DOWN, without any slouching.

6. If the correct push is made, the free foot should come off the ice, when it is behind you, turned out and in line with the heel of the tracing foot as indicated in Rule 1. All that remains is to give a little extra turn out and to point the toe. When pushing backwards, however, the pushing foot does not come off the ice already turned out because the pushing foot turns in for the push. Therefore, as the pushing foot comes off the ice it is necessary immediately to turn out the foot and point the toe, making sure the free heel remains in line with the toe of the tracing foot.

Glossary of Terms used in this Book

TRACING FOOT. The foot on which you are standing.

FREE FOOT OR FREE LEG. The foot which is off the ice, having just completed the push.

CROSSED STEP. When the free foot, which is to become the new tracing foot, is placed on the ice either in front or behind the existing tracing foot.

CHASSÉ. A movement whereby the free foot is placed on the ice beside the tracing foot, the tracing foot being lifted off the ice without moving forward or backward prior to replacement on the ice.

CROSS CHASSÉ. A chassé in which the free foot is placed on the ice crossed behind the skating foot when skating forward, or crossed in front when skating backward.

RUN. Where the free foot passes the tracing foot in a running action, the tracing foot coming off the ice in a following movement.

LOBE. A complete semi-circle.

ARABESQUE. Where the body is horizontal with the free foot approximately level with the head. More commonly known on the ice as a *spiral*, though this is not in fact actually correct because a spiral really refers to skating a circle which decreases in radius.

PIROUETTE. A spiral decreasing in radius until the free foot can be stretched behind the skater and the toe placed on the ice to form a pivot point for the skating foot to circle round.

MOHAWK. A two footed turn from forward to backward, the forward edge being skated by one foot and the backward edge by the other.

140

OPEN MOHAWK. When the new tracing foot is placed on the ice to the inside of the existing tracing foot, approximately by the instep, the free foot coming off the ice behind the new tracing foot.

CLOSED MOHAWK. When the new tracing foot is placed on to the ice to the outside of the existing tracing foot at the heel, the free foot coming off the ice in front of the new tracing foot.

CHOCTAW. The same as the Mohawk, with this difference: whereas the forward and backward edges of the mohawk are either both outside or inside edges, in the choctaw, if the forward edge is inside, the backward is outside and *vice versa*.

OPEN OR CLOSED CHOCTAW. The same as for the Mohawk.

X.B. Crossed behind.

X.F. Crossed in front.

X.R. Cross roll.

R.F.O. Right Forward Outside Edge.

L.F.O. Left Forward Outside Edge.

R.B.O. Right Backward Outside Edge.

L.B.O. Left Backward Outside Edge. 'The last letter represents the edge – 0 outside – I inside.'

R.F.O.T.B.I. Right Forward Outside Three Backward Inside Edge.

L.F.O.T.B.I. Left Forward Outside Three Backward Inside Edge.

L.F.O.R.B.O. Left Forward Outside Rocker Backward Outside Edge.

AXIS. The beginner will understand the meaning of the word axis in relation to ice dancing better by giving a little thought to the fact that all dances progress continuously around the rink in either an anti-clockwise or clockwise direction – in the main anti-clockwise. If, therefore, we divide the rink longtitudinally in half, it will be seen that we dance down one side, round the end of the rink and up the other side. To assist us in the better formation of the lobes and edges, we draw another line – imaginary, of course – half way between the centre line of the rink and the barrier, continuing down the length of the rink and around the ends making a continuous line round the rink. This is known as the Continuous or Long axis.

We use yet another Axis which is called the Transverse or Short Axis, this is a line which cuts across the rink or at right angles to the Continuous Axis.

COMING BACK ON YOUR TRACK. Failing to proceed along the Transverse Axis by over curving the edge and allowing the edge to run back into the circle.

Dance Holds

HAND IN HAND. Used in free dancing where both partners face in the same direction, with the arms extended, the two bodies and arms forming a straight line, not a V.

CLOSED OR WALTZ. The partners dance squarely in front of each other. The man's right hand on his partner's back by the shoulder blade, while his left arm is extended with his hand at about shoulder level, his right elbow raised to a similar height. The lady's left arm rests on the man's right arm, her elbow on top of his, her forearm resting lightly on the upper part of the man's right arm, while her right arm is extended to co-inside with the man's left arm, both elbows being very slightly dropped, to avoid a 'stiff' appearance.

OPEN OR FOXTROT. The hand and arm positions are the same as for the Waltz, the lady bringing her left side a little towards the man while he brings his right side slightly towards the lady, both then being able to skate in the same direction.

OUTSIDE OR TANGO. Partner's skate in opposite directions, one skating forward while the other skates backward, hip to hip, the man being to the right or left.

KILIAN. Partners face in the same direction, the lady on the man's right, the man's shoulder slightly behind the lady's left, the hips and shoulders forming a parallel line. The lady's left arm is extended across the front of the man, her left hand being held by the man's left hand. The man's right arm is extended across the back of the lady, both right hands are resting on the lady's right hip.